LIVING IN THE SPIRIT

LIVING IN THE SPIRIT

A HANDBOOK ON
CATHOLIC CHARISMATIC CHRISTIANITY

by
James E. Byrne

PAULIST PRESS
New York / Paramus / Toronto

NIHIL OBSTAT
Rev. Harold Bumpus, Th.D.
Censor Deputatus

IMPRIMATUR
✠Charles B. McLaughlin, D.D.
Bishop of St. Petersburg

August 12, 1975

The Nihil Obstat and Imprimatur are official declarations that a book or pamphlet is free of doctrinal or moral error. No implication is contained therein that those who have granted the Nihil Obstat and Imprimatur agree with the contents, opinions or statements expressed.

Library of Congress
Catalog Card Number: 75-28628

ISBN: 0-8091-1902-1

Published by Paulist Press
Editorial Office: 1865 Broadway, N.Y., N.Y. 10023
Business Office: 400 Sette Drive, Paramus, N.J. 07652

Printed and bound in the
United States of America

Contents

To
Fr. Edward D. O'Connor, C.S.C.,
whose deep loyalty to the Spirit
and love of the Church
have been a source
of light and hope to many.

Preface

It is necessary to justify the introduction of another book into the vast flood of charismatic literature. This book is offered to those who have received the "baptism in the Holy Spirit" and are involved in the charismatic movement of the Holy Spirit commonly called the Charismatic Renewal. It seeks to treat under one cover the principal issues and challenges which face charismatics in incorporating this experience into their lives in a fruitful way. It treats these issues in a practical manner while carefully seeking to lay a balanced theoretical foundation. Without such a foundation, a charismatic is left to the mercies of his own experience and that of others. And at times this experience can be a fickle guide.

The "baptism in the Holy Spirit" is an initiation into a movement of grace. An answer to prayer, it does not of itself solve the problems of life but releases energies and offers special graces by which these problems can be faced and eventually overcome. It is of the greatest importance that charismatics understand this effect and the difference between such a work of grace and a panacea. The "baptism in the Holy Spirit" makes possible great strides in the human, psychological, and spiritual dimensions of a person's life. Viewed in this way, it is more a challenge than a solution. The "baptism in the Holy Spirit" and the movement which it introduces pose questions themselves which also must be faced if this work of grace is to be fully integrated into a person's life.

This book addresses the basic issues of what the "baptism in the Holy Spirit" is and is not and of what an adequate response to it is. It also faces the difficult questions with which all charismatics must wrestle such as the need to develop a deep spiritual life, the charismatic gifts of the Spirit and their function, the leadings of the Spirit and guidance, and charismatic community and its relation to the Church.

These issues are addressed with a sense of urgency. My approach is based on the conviction that the free response of individual charismatics will determine the fruitfulness of their own experience and ultimately the effectiveness of the movement as a force for Christian renewal. Growth requires faithfulness to the Spirit and the experience of charismatics by now must surely convince us that such faithfulness is no easy matter. What we deal with here is the loving desire of God to make us whole in him, to unite us in him, and to renew us. The interior and exterior forces at work to thwart his intention do not cease with the "baptism in the Holy Spirit." They put on a new face. Consequently, charismatics, if they are not to be Pharisees of the twentieth century, must seek to base their response to the Spirit's work on a sober recognition of the challenges and difficulties that face them. Above all, they must recognize the need for a deep personal commitment to the continual interior transformation which the Spirit seeks to accomplish.

It is to this deeper level of the Spirit's work, the more serious issues of the renewal, and the need for a serious response that this book seeks to awaken charismatics. Pope Paul VI indicated this need in his address to charismatics on May 19, 1975, the text of which is given at the end of this book. Speaking of Pentecost, he called it "a day of joy but also a day of resolve and determination: to open ourselves to the Holy Spirit, to remove what is opposed to his action, and to proclaim, in the Christian authenticity of our daily lives, that Jesus is Lord." Only to the extent that the renewal of the Spirit touches our innermost self, and demonstrates itself in the affairs of our daily lives, will it be effective.

I therefore invite the reader to treat this book as an invitation to a spiritual quest or inquiry and, like Mary, to ponder all these things lovingly in his or her heart (cf. Lk. 2:51). To do so, we must ask the Spirit for his special gift of wisdom. Let us not hesitate, either, to ask Mary to pray for us for this gift, since she is the seat of wisdom, having borne the Wisdom of God (cf. 1 Cor 1:24).

I also must acknowledge with gratitude the assistance of the following people whose advice and encouragement made this book possible: Mrs. Joan Blackey, Mr. and Mrs. William Callaghan and the members of the Spirit of God community whose hospitality to us was a sign of deep charity, Mr. and Mrs. Michael Difato, Sr. Amata Fabbro, O.P., Rev. Earnest Larkin, O. Carm., Mr. and Mrs. Marquardt, Michelle Morrison, Rev. Edward O'Connor, C.S.C., Barbara Schlemon, and Mrs. Judy Tydings. Friends who assisted with typing were: my mother, Mrs. Grace Byrne, Mrs. Kathy Kolinski, Mrs. Doris Meagher, Mrs. Jeanne Morrison, and Lucille Doychak. Above all, I must acknowledge the patient and loving support of my wife Maria who encouraged me in putting this material together.

I
"Receive the Spirit"

"Power," writes St. Paul; "demonstration of the Spirit and power" (1 Cor. 2:4-5). "Wait," commands our Lord, "until you are clothed with power from on high" (Lk. 24:49). "When you believed," asks St. Paul of the Ephesians, "did you receive the Holy Spirit?" (Acts 19:2). "If anyone thirst," says our Lord, "let him come to me and drink. He who believes in me, as Scripture has said, 'Out of his heart shall flow rivers of living water'" (Jn. 7:37-38). "Now this," writes St. John, "he said about the Spirit, which those who believed in him were to receive; for as yet the Spirit had not been given because Jesus was not yet glorified" (Jn. 7:39).

Many people would respond to these verses as did the Ephesians, and say, "We have never even heard. . . ." (Acts 19:2). Others, though, would respond with a thrill and an inner movement of the heart. They have tasted of the waters of life flowing from Christ, have been clothed with power, have received the gift of the Holy Spirit. Some of these people are charismatics. It is to them that this book is addressed.

The charismatic movement has recently and quite suddenly emerged as a major spiritual force in the Christian world.[1] It has been a vessel through which the needs and longings of many have been awakened and, to some measure, answered. It is a movement based not on a shared ideology or on common social or political principles. Rather, its basis is a common response to an initiative made by God in many lives and hearts.

Although it has some of the trappings of a movement in the sense of organization and doctrine, at its essence is a personal response to a work of grace. The Holy Spirit is at work through it, moving hearts in love toward God and others.

The most important question for someone to ask after receiving the baptism in the Holy Spirit is: "What happened?" Although most people do not raise their heads from prayer with this question on their lips, they do reflect upon it and formulate some explanation. In light of this understanding, the experience within either unfolds and deepens, taking on a depth and luster as time passes, or else it withers and fades. Because there has been little time in which to formulate and propose a satisfactory general explanation of the experience, it is possible for the experience to be less meaningful than it can be.

Before we turn our attention to this experience, we must settle on a name. It is commonly referred to as the "baptism of the Holy Spirit." This name is taken from Scripture. At first glance, it adequately describes what occurs. Upon reflection, however, it can be seen that when our Lord speaks of the baptism in the Holy Spirit, he refers to several things, including the pentecostal event and the culmination of his work in the parousia as well as the multiple workings of the Spirit in the life of an individual.[2] To apply such a term to this experience does an injustice, blurring both the experience and our Lord's meaning. The experience is a special and wonderful work of the Spirit. Jesus probably meant this and much more in his promised baptism of the Spirit. Moreover, the name is too easily confused with the sacrament of baptism, which it is not. As a result, I have chosen to refer to the experience commonly called the "baptism in the Holy Spirit" as the charismatic experience of the Holy Spirit.

A. The Reason for an Explanation of the Charismatic Experience

Perhaps a lengthy inquiry into the meaning and place of the charismatic experience needs to be justified in a book intended for charismatics. After all one who is a charismatic has received this experience. Doesn't a person who has received an experience understand it? What need is there for further explanation of it?

There is much justification for the first of these questions. The experience frequently is accompanied by an understanding which is wonderful. I have seen examples of individuals untrained in theology and spiritually uninformed who have responded in awkward situations to problems posed by or about the experience with a delicacy and wisdom that could only come from an inner light. Many times, for instance, I have seen unlettered souls respond to searing and telling arguments by knowledgeable professionals in ways reminiscent of the scene in the temple in which Jesus confounded the doctors (Lk. 2:41ff). Or again, I have heard individuals, scarcely embarked upon a serious Christianity, address groups in such a way that all marveled at their wisdom (cf. Lk. 4:22). I have likewise witnessed mere "babes in Christ" traverse unscathed a veritable minefield of temptations or errors, led in a privileged way, step by step, by the Holy Spirit. Nor do I believe that this remarkable divine presence is rare.

In less dramatic situations, the same observations hold true. Upon receiving the charismatic experience, an individual enters into a new dimension of his relationship with God, frequently characterized by a deeper awareness of God's presence and leadings. It seems to dawn upon a new charismatic that God can be served and pleased in the little affairs that fill the day. Especially in the days immediately following the reception of the charismatic experience, there are often numerous manifestations of God's special presence and leadings. Inspirations to speak to someone, to pray, to do an act are clothed with deep significance, while passages of the Bible, prayer, or even coincidences take on a new aspect in the light of the experience. In these early days, then, God is present with a power and certainty which serves as a security against doubt and mistake. Of course, there can be self-delusion, but in my experience this is infrequent. The greater majority of those whom I have known to have received the charismatic experience of the Holy Spirit were blessed in similar ways.

This inner light which can be called an intuitive understanding is a fragile gift, however. It requires an individual's cooperation with an extraordinary grace, is subject to withdrawal, and has its limitations. Personal disloyalty to this grace or to God can shatter this inner sense. For example, selfishness, pride, hatred, or ambition can cause this light to wither. A failure to be loyal to it can have the same effect. Furthermore, it usually is, after a time, withdrawn to some extent.

At this point, we will digress for a moment to treat the possibility of an extraordinary grace, once given, being withdrawn. Such an idea, at first, may strike an odd note. It seems contradictory for a grace to be given and then withdrawn where no sin or disloyalty has occurred. The difficulty which such a notion presents requires closer examination. It is an important spiritual principle with far-reaching ramifications for a charismatic spirituality. Its application to the graces by which the charismatic experience is intuitively understood provides a good occasion for examination. This grace is one of many which seem to accompany the reception of the charismatic experience. For most charismatics, this is a honeymoon time when they are lifted into God's presence in a special way. Troubles seem to fall away, prayer comes easily, and priorities are seen in sharp perspective. It is not at all unusual for works of grace to begin in such a way. This is a time in which to taste God's fullness. This taste, however, is really only a foretaste of the fullness which is to come. It is a time which ends. Although the ending can be hastened by sin or disloyalty, it is simplistic to attribute it to evil or infidelity as if it would otherwise continue always. There is a pattern applicable to all of God's workings operative here. In simple terms, it runs from honeymoon to purification to illumination and deeper unity. In great and small matters, this pattern repeats itself. With spiritual milk God sustains a new spiritual birth, comforting it close to himself. At some point, though, it must be weaned.

This pattern of foretaste/struggle/fulfillment is typified in the broadest outlines by the story of God's people, Israel. For them, the time of birth was the exodus. God led them by cloud and fire, feeding them with manna and quail, slaking their thirst with water from the rock. Throughout this time, he cared for them as his children. When they entered the promised land, however, the pattern of his work changed. The manna and quail ceased, his leadership became less tangible, and the victories were less obvious. Throughout these centuries, he tried and tested them, preparing them for a fulfillment in Christ which was beyond their fondest imaginations in those first days. It would be shortsighted to attribute the change which took place in the promised land as due only to their sins. They sinned in the desert too, yet God's special presence did not fail them (cf. Ex. 33:12-16). The change in the mode of God's work was due to his desire to prepare them for something more wonderful.

To be sure, this pattern can be traced on a smaller scale in many of the events which occurred during this period. The pattern painted in such broad strokes applies to the honeymoon graces of the charismatic experience as well. They end because of God's plan to perfect and purify. An individual should not be frightened or despair when this occurs or conclude that his relationship with God has "ended." Such an event is a prelude to further growth and a normal part of the economy of grace.

To close our digression, the intuitive understanding accompanying the charismatic experience is also liable to be withdrawn. Even where it is not, or there is no disloyalty, the understanding has its limitations. Many of the very people to whom I referred above found themselves dumbfounded at times. In some situations, too, the inner leadings are unreliable due to temptations, our emotions, or other factors. That is, this gentle sense can be so disquieted as to make it unreliable. God does not give it as a complete, comprehensive, or exclusive means by which to guide an individual. It is a gift, can be very important, and should be taken seriously. It is, however, analogous to our conscience which is reliable when fed with the truth, but which can become twisted or distorted. This inner sense needs to be coupled with common sense and revelation as understood by the Christian people before it is reliable as a guide. In other words, a prayerful, reflective attempt to understand the charismatic experience serves to flesh out the intuitive understanding, strengthen its weaknesses, eliminate its mistakes, emphasize its strengths and expand its horizons. It is a mistake to believe that experience explains itself or that a person, having had an experience, necessarily understands it. The realm of experience differs from that of understanding. It is possible to reflect on experience, relate it to revelation, theology, and the Christian experience, and deepen one's insight into the experience.

The emphasis placed upon the role of reflective, prayerful thought here may come as a surprise to some. There is a tendency to regard the two as incompatible, which affects the approach of many to the charismatic renewal. Although some of the issues involved are dealt with in Chapter 4 in reference to guidance, they can also be fruitfully considered in the context of an approach to the charismatic experience. They are important because they tend to influence one's attitude to the entire renewal and many of its aspects. What we are trying to identify is the underlying basis of a tendency expressed in many different ways. The tendency also has some important truths at its basis, but here we are concerned with isolating one theory which I believe to be shallow.

The approach places an exclusive emphasis upon the experiential as the primary means by which God can be known, loved, or obeyed. In this line of thought, experience of God through encounters such as the charismatic experience are the only true revelations of God. Experiential communications in the form of leadings, revelations, or coincidence are the principal way of knowing his will. In this approach, planning, reflections, or consistency are thrown to the wind before a super-spiritual spontaneity. In following the Spirit's leadings, there is to be no reflection, prayers, or evaluation. Such things only undermine faith. This approach rapidly gives rise to a system wherein every check is a test or trial, every sane council a denial of faith, and every failure a confirmation. Taken to its extreme, such a tendency offers no ground upon which rational men can communicate. It is based on the genuine insight that a person must be loyal to the leadings of the Spirit. The fundamental weakness is in equating a blind response to experiential impulse with following the Spirit's leading and in discounting the role of reason and common sense. Through this approach, an essentially subjective world view is created wherein fantasy cannot be distinguished from fact. To be sure, such a tendency cannot always be easily distinguished from a true loyalty to the Spirit. Men of God and Christ himself were called at times to throw human prudence to the wind. Their life style and habit, however, differed from the one with which we are concerned. They did not despise reason. They obeyed authority. They heard the Word of God in other ways besides their own private revelation. Exposed, this tendency appears more like a weather vane running before whatever happens to blow than a loving response to God.

It is reinforced by various things, however, which disguise it. There is a value placed on spontaneity today. The one who can be "free" is the one who is spiritual. Somehow, this impression of the super-spiritual man impresses itself upon charismatics. In an era of intense life styles, such an approach offers a tremendous release as well. It appears as an answer to modern life's frustrations. It is also reinforced by some sloppy habits of charismatics whose speech and spirituality, if taken by themselves, depict a spiritual life in which God seems to be constantly on the "hot line" with daily, if not hourly, messages. Such language ignores the process of discernment and reflection necessary to understand God's will. Furthermore, charismatics often fall into the regrettable habit of citing God as the principal and direct authority for something they themselves think should be done. This substitution is rarely done deliberately. It comes from a failure to clearly articulate the difference between a rational process, by which God's will is sought through reflection upon certain data, including supernatural signs, and a blind irrational response to an impulse.

All of these tendencies are further clouded by a characteristic of the renewal which I call the "emperor's clothes syndrome." It affects individuals and groups. Its name comes from the famous tale which describes it so well. In the fabled kingdom, the emperor was promised a new suit, more magnificent than that of any other ruler. The basic ingredient was gold which was refined into a fabric so wondrous that only the wise and discerning could behold it. Of course everyone, being wise and discerning, saw it—everyone, that is, but a little child. On the day it was finished, as the tailors hastily departed with the gold, the emperor paraded in his birthday suit. The admiring remarks of his subjects were cut short when our little child cried out: "He doesn't have anything on!" In a flash, everyone realized what had happened.

Every charismatic community needs one such child. Not wanting to seem unspiritual, many times charismatics hold their tongue, tolerating pure nonsense. Indeed, I have witnessed situations in which most people in a room felt uncomfortable with something obviously off base, where all responded positively, and yet later confided their uneasiness. Because of these characteristics, the super-spiritual tendency of which we have spoken is reinforced.

An important distinction must be made, however. There is a process of trial and error by which a new charismatic seeks to grow. In this process, many mistakes are made. Few charismatics would not turn red in embarrassment over some incident. Devils "discerned" in antagonists, spectacular prayer on a street corner, and following a wild impulse are but a few with which I am acquainted. Immature Christians will make such mistakes and there is no reason for undue alarm. Indeed, the difference between normal, healthy growth and the super-spiritual tendency is that with the latter there never is any learning. The process of testing and evaluation of leadings never takes place. There is no development of criteria by which past experiences, common sense, and right reason, enlightened by revelation understood by the Church, are brought to focus upon a given impulse. It is in this ability to prayerfully reflect that a deep response to the charismatic experience is distinguished. A charismatic is indeed charismatic, but he does not distain common sense. He does not make a cult out of blindly following impulses. At its worse, this tendency turns the charismatic dimension into a game of magic, hardly distinguishable from common superstitions. At its best, the tendency can encourage a beginner in living by faith. However, the price of retarded growth and a shallow spirituality is too high to pay. This tendency will not hold up under the floods and rains certain to come (cf. Mt. 6:24ff). It is no foundation upon which to build a spiritual life.

Because this tendency first raises its head in a rejection of rational reflection of the charismatic experience, we address it here. There is much benefit in reflecting upon the experience. A balanced approach to the experience lays a basis for a healthy and solid approach to the renewal. The habits of thought and spirituality learned in the immediate wake of the charismatic experience have a major effect on subsequent spirituality. The way in which one considers the experience itself is of even greater consequence. It is important to build an adequate framework in which to understand the experience and its implications. Whether consciously or not, attitudes and opinions are formed. It is far better that they be shaped in the clear light of prayerful reflection than by happenstance. Because a charismatic conception of the experience is so vital, we will now attempt to propose such a framework.

B. A Context in Which To Understand the Charismatic Experience

At the outset it is tempting to see the charismatic as the Pentecostal experience and to close one's eyes to the ages that separate the early Church from the present. This temptation is understandable. The power and wonder of the charismatic experience bring to life for many the events and occurrences described in Acts. No longer does the work of Peter with Cornelius or the conversion of thousands on Pentecost seem mysterious. Having experienced for themselves the power of the Spirit, charismatics find the events recorded understandable. It must be recognized that what they have experienced is, in a sense, the same thing. Though separated by time and civilization, the same Spirit is at work to accomplish the same results. The inevitable question arises sooner or later: Why did the Church lose this experience? In the first glow of the experience, it seems impossible that the Church should have ever slipped from it.

It is, of course, a temptation for every enthusiastic movement to see itself as a direct heir of the experience of the early Church. Resolutions thereupon are made that never again will this insight be lost and a subtle attitude of superiority is formed toward Christians of past ages and others not blessed with the experience. Immaturity and self-confidence can easily fuel this tendency. It usually represents an inability to appreciate the depth of God's plan and of his love and to take into account men's stubbornness. Men in other ages and at other times had similar longings and zeal for God. There is no age of the Church in which such longings were not present or realized. Nor is there any age of the Church in which these plans and hopes did not, to some extent at least, become bogged down. The history of the Church is indeed littered with the tales of those who would have started anew, seeing for themselves the mystery of Christianity only to find that over time their work was indistinguishable from others.

Of course the early Church should appeal to Christians of all ages as a model and ideal. It offers a standard by which the Church and Christians can judge their loyalty and devotion. In this honeymoon time, so close to our Lord's words and steps, the

Church was bathed with the bridegroom's memory. But the Holy Spirit was given for all times and is with the Church in every age (cf. Jn. 14:16). In God's plan for the Church, there was a need for growth and development if the knowledge of Christ was to come to all men. Over the past twenty centuries Christians have struggled with challenges and opportunities, at times seeming to lapse into a lethargy, only to reawaken to the graces of God with even greater vigor.

Although this is not the place to attempt an interpretation of Church history, it must be noted that throughout this history God has raised up forces of renewal. Some have succeeded and some have not. Likewise there have been times in which his work was not as apparent. This pattern is operative as well in the life of an individual. There are periods of dryness or trial. It is crippling to fail to see that God uses both phases to draw men to a more singlehearted love and knowledge of himself. For those in the throes of renewal, it is hard to realize that these graces are not always given. When these graces cease, however, they cannot be forced to resume by human efforts or gadgets. They are a gift from God. They cannot be presumed or taken for granted at any time or in any era.

From this discussion, it should be apparent that the attitude which a person develops toward this charismatic experience will influence his attitude toward other things of God as well. Therefore, the means by which he conceives and expresses his opinions is of the utmost importance. The Church has appreciated the importance of such formulations from its earliest days. The epistles of Paul, for example, take issue with those who viewed the revelation in Christ as subordinate to the law. Throughout the ages of the Church division, disputes, and schism attended divergent formulations of God's works. Although often a sad commentary on the foibles of Christians, they also bear witness to the importance attached by Christians to the way in which they express their faith. The importance of such formulations is clearly recognized in the charismatic renewal as well. Gradually an ideology is emerging which explains the charismatic experience and interprets its meaning. Some charismatic communities, properly sensing the danger of unbalanced teaching, have sought to screen and test teachings and formulations. Indeed at times, there is a rigidity of control unknown at present throughout most of the Church. It does matter how people understand their experience and how they relate it to other aspects of Christianity. The reason is obvious. The conceptual framework in which they approach something will dictate to a considerable extent their response to it. For example, the attitude conveyed in regard to the history of God's work will have major implications on a new charismatic. Especially at the time of such a tremendous personal upheaval, people are susceptible to any influence. If a person is told by one he respects that the Church has in the past been seriously disloyal to God's grace and lost the Spirit, that will affect his approach to the Church.

It does matter, then, that the manner in which the charismatic experience of the Holy Spirit is explained is sufficiently broad and deep to offer a healthy framework for a full Christian life. A perspective which looks no farther than one powerful experience is inadequate. So is one which fails to take into account the stages of growth and patterns of development necessary for growth. It is to be expected, of course, that any new movement would attempt to some degree to fashion a theoretical framework based on its success and experience and be wary of formulations which appear powerless. This tendency must be balanced, however, by a healthy respect for the manifold workings of the Spirit and a deep love for the mind of the Church. To adequately consider the charismatic experience with sufficient breadth in light of these things, it is necessary to approach it from a double perspective rather than taking the experience itself as a starting point. Consequently, we will examine (1) the work of the Spirit in the life of an individual and (2) the social aspects of the Spirit's work. In light of our reflections, we will then examine the experience itself and its implications (Part C).

1. The Work of the Spirit in the Life of an Individual

Although, as we will explain later, some charismatics have already received a deep spiritual formation, the greatest impact of the movement is on those who have not lived a deep or serious Christian life. As a result, we will focus upon the initial stage of the Christian life.

Some have sought to isolate the essential element of what it means to become a Christian. Simply put, Protestant thought has tended to emphasize the act of faith, often discounting sacrament or even experience. Other Protestants would insist on an intimate experiential personal encounter with Jesus as the essential element of being a Christian. Pentecostals see the necessary experience as being the infilling of the Holy Spirit rather than the encounter with Christ. There is a sense in which Catholics have tended to emphasize the sacrament of baptism in this process. These insights deserve respect. To some extent, however, considerable attention given to these differences obscures an important dimension of becoming a Christian. It is a process. Rarely will anyone be so fool-hardy as to claim that once initiated—however one sees that as accomplished—there is no need for instruction and formation. The well-placed emphasis upon the efficacy of the sacrament of baptism does not hinder Catholics, for example, from treating with considerable import the training of the young. Evangelicals who are the first to claim that an encounter with Christ is the mark of a Christian will also be the first to urge that a Christian attend Bible courses or Scripture sessions to deepen his understanding of the faith. In other words, the emphasis upon particular aspects of initiation or their efficacy can obscure the pastoral realities. These realities in fact govern the conduct and to some degree the fruitfulness of an effort at initiation into the Christian life.

Viewed from a pastoral perspective, one becomes a Christian by means of a process which takes some length of time. Like a great river, it has beginnings which are often difficult to trace and many tributaries which run together until it becomes a great body of water. The Spirit does not leave unturned any aspect of a man's life and draws together many threads in an intricate pattern. The purpose of the Spirit's work is to present men with the truth about Christ and to offer them a choice. Once the choice has been made, the Spirit works to reveal him to them and to draw them closer to him. This is the work of a lifetime. A wholehearted love of God and others is not easily attained. In any person's life, it comes by way of much suffering, trial, and sacrifice. Our Lord's disciples may have opted for him in an instant, but only he who endured would be saved.

In Christian cultures this process is less evident because God's grace is able to work in a more hidden manner. Exposed to sources of grace in a multitude of ways, a person's love of God can gently be fanned into flame. In non-Christian cultural situations where Christ is not regarded as Lord and Christianity is not generally accepted as an ideal, the process for those who are not will be more drastic.

Although considerable attention has been given to pastoral technique in a Christian and non-Christian culture, there is little understanding of how to approach the post-Christian culture of twentieth-century America. The methodology of the missions, while not entirely appropriate, may offer a better guide than tactics whose basic presumption is that almost everyone believes in Christ. Since the Church is moving from a Christian culture, its orientation is suited to a very different situation. It is able, for example, to form and guide Christians who are interested, but does not understand how to stir up that interest. Such tools of formation are useless when no one wants to be formed. No longer do the multiple aspects of Christian culture which once surrounded Catholics serve to nurture and nourish a nascent faith until it buds into a living hunger for Christ. In such an environment, it was not as necessary for the Church to deliberately cultivate a spiritual awareness. In an environment such as that in America today, it is necessary to do so because almost all of the means that God could have used to regularly awaken interest have dried up. As a result, we are discovering what our Protestant friends have discovered before us, that the erosion of a religious culture requires a deliberate effort to awaken individuals to the reality of the spiritual life. There are many individuals who are spiritually asleep. They have either lost touch with the life of grace or never been exposed to it. In such a situation, the process by which one comes to an active and serious love of God will generally be more pronounced and dramatic.

It is important to realize that this process can be encouraged. There is a tendency to regard spiritual growth as something too individualistic to admit of mass techniques. There is much truth in such a position. However, a distinction must be drawn between the advanced stages of the spiritual life and the early ones. In fact, it must be recognized that it is possible to create and use systematic pastoral tools which offer the Spirit a means of awakening an individual spiritually. This is a radical insight for many, although the Church's history is not without examples of the effectiveness of such methods. The Life in the Spirit seminars have been singularly successful as a method in the charismatic renewal. The effectiveness of these tools, however, should not be allowed to obscure the important truth that initiation into the full Christian life is a process. One dramatic event or systematic course may accelerate the process but does not bypass it. This is important because they are much more artificial than a Catholic culture and, in order to be fully effective, require follow-up.

Therefore, it is of great importance for charismatics to appreciate the nature of this work of initiation and to grasp the elements of the process. No attempt at specifying these elements will be entirely satisfactory. One system which has the merit of being based on scriptural examples will suffice here. Because this process varies in its particulars, any given individual may be able to mark with precision only parts of what we describe. Some elements are explicit, while others may occur over time and less obviously. Other analyses are possible, of course. The scriptural examples, however, are so familiar that they offer, I believe, an excellent starting point.

Five elements can be identified in the various stories in Acts. They are: (1) proclamation of the Word; (2) repentance; (3) faith; (4) sacramental baptism; (5) an experience of the Holy Spirit. It is my opinion that each of these elements was considered an integral part of the process of becoming a Christian by the early Church. For the sake of simplicity, we will call this process one of initiation-conversion. It is necessary, for example, for an individual to have heard the Word of life in order to believe (Rom. 10:14). The role of the apostles was that of witnesses whose duty was to proclaim the message which they had received. Without having heard this message, men cannot believe. It may too easily be assumed today that men have heard the Gospel. The proclamation of it, as the recently developed theology of preaching seeks to emphasize, is, however, a work of grace. There is a proclamation by which the whole saving work of God in Christ is set forth. It cannot be assumed today, especially among the young, that they have heard this message. Likewise, the other elements are integral parts of becoming a Christian. Several are obvious. That one must repent, believe, and be baptized is a familiar formula (cf. Acts 2:38). Familiar, too, is the adage: "And you shall receive the gift of the Holy Spirit." This reception of the gift of the Holy Spirit is, however, not always recognized as a distinct aspect of the initiation-conversion process. It is often confused with the fundamental indwelling of the Spirit by which one is in Christ. The early Christians failed to make the theological distinctions which we are able to make regarding the imparting of the Holy Spirit. They understood that it was fundamental to being a Christian for one to have the Spirit of Christ (Rom. 8:9). They also knew the presence of the Spirit as a distinct experience in their lives (cf. Acts 19:1-6; Gal. 3:1-5). A careful reading of Acts or of the epistles makes it apparent that the early Christians spoke from the perspective of a first-hand experience of the Holy Spirit. They did not carefully distinguish between the indwelling presence of the Spirit and an experience of the Spirit, or if they did, it is not apparent.

These two aspects of the Spirit's work are distinct or distinguishable, however. The experience of the Holy Spirit is an experiential awareness of the Spirit which causes a spiritual sensitivity to the presence of the Spirit and openness to the charismatic workings of the Spirit. It is not necessarily that fundamental gift of the Spirit by which one becomes a Christian. This is recognizable in the stories in Acts. The Samaritans had received the Word of God and been baptized (proclamation, repentance, act of faith, and baptism in our schema). It is foolish to maintain that the Holy Spirit was not with them until later when Peter and John came down from Jerusalem. What they received at that time was an experience of the Holy Spirit (Acts 8:4-17). What occurred when the Spirit "fell" on the believers was an experience so impressive that Simon offered to buy the power. The experience of the Spirit, then, is an important element in the process of becoming a Christian. It is an event or experience which happens at a given time or over a period and which can be identified. A person can be a Christian and not have had such an experience. A person cannot know the fullness of Christ's gift, however, without having had it.

Although the experience of the Spirit is frequently equated with other elements of initiation-conversion, it is itself a separate element. In some stories, it does occur simultaneously with other elements. This is true, though, of all of the elements at one point or another. Faith and baptism in some stories occur simultaneously; in others, they follow each other. In the incident at Samaria or the scene at Cornelius' house (Acts 10:44ff), however, the experience of the Spirit is distinct. It could be suggested that as a pastoral tool this experience be equated with the sacrament of confirmation which is itself a sacrament of initiation. Such an equation, however, leads to a fundamental confusion between the sacramental order and the order of experience. It is possible for the two to occur simultaneously, and it could be argued, for pastoral reasons, that they should be emphasized together. Whether it is wise to link the two, or to expose young children to the charismatic experience, is beyond the scope of this inquiry. Even if the two were united for pastoral reasons, the distinction would remain.

In this light, it may be well to note a temptation which often occurs to theorists. Sometimes, an ideal order or formula by which the process of initiation-conversion *should* occur is proposed. For example, the suggested order may run: proclamation, repentance, act of faith, experience of the Holy Spirit, and baptism. It may be tied to notions of a ritual or liturgical pattern. In reality, there is no such pattern and no basis by which an ideal one can be established. The examples available in Acts are noteworthy for their lack of any consistency. Recognition of the haphazardness of this process is important because the existence of apostolic tools can give an impression that such an order should exist. For example, in the Life in the Spirit seminar, attention is given one week to a personal encounter with Christ, to repentance the next week, etc. The fact that attention is paid to these areas will not necessarily mean that they have or should happen at this time or in this order in the life of an individual. The Spirit blows where he wills, draws hearts according to his own wisdom, and will not be reduced in his actions to our methods or formulas. They do have a value and role, but become obstacles when they are imposed without sensitivity for individual problems and situations. It must also be recognized that the process of initiation-conversion need not happen within a short sequence. The factors which will influence the time necessary to reach Christian maturity cannot be set forth plainly. Many are intangible. They represent a combination of ingredients such as loyalty to God's will, purity of conscience, human maturity, and God's will. It is sufficient for our purposes here to note that the process, even after having received the charismatic experience, may take many years. Even where the experience appears to be a threshold for Christian maturity, it is most often preceded by years of hidden workings of the Spirit so that what is seen is only the tip of the iceberg.

We have proposed several elements by which the process of initiation-conversion can be identified and understood. In this framework, they are necessary prerequisites for further stages of Christian growth such as the purgative or illuminative stages. Cast in a very crude framework, we have said that they are necessary for a basic Christian maturity. Paul and the author of Hebrews speak in a rough fashion of such a distinction (cf. 1 Cor. 3:1-2; Heb. 5:11-14). The elements of these further stages do not concern us here. It is rather our purpose to identify the much more nebulous stage which is a prerequisite for spiritual maturity. This stage does exist and is more complex than may have been imagined. It is a process by which an individual's mind, heart and spirit are opened to the Word of God. It is a time of reorientation in which a whole new world view is formulated, a spirituality formed, and a new series of social values and relationships forged. The process can be encouraged by deliberate pastoral tools. These tools, however, do not work automatically and must be used with sensitivity and wisdom. One element of the process which is of great interest to charismatics is the experience of the Holy Spirit. For them, the experiential order has often been the starting point of a serious interest in Christian growth or at least has served to accelerate their awareness of the spiritual life. An evaluation of the entire process by which an individual comes to a living and mature relationship with Christ provides an important perspective for the charismatic. It is important because energies released by this experience must be directed toward building an adequate foundation. To a considerable extent, it is upon this foundation that any further growth in the spiritual life will rest. To fail to recognize the entire process of initiation-conversion and to seek to orient new charismatics to this broader perspective is irresponsible.

In setting this perspective, however, we have not directly considered the relationship between the elements identified and the charismatic experience. A logical question at this point would be: "Is the experience of the Holy Spirit of which we have spoken the charismatic experience (or baptism in the Holy Spirit)?" The answer, which is a somewhat puzzling "yes" and "no" (that is, it depends upon the person's situation), will become clearer when we have considered the other perspective necessary to understand the experience. It is impossible to appreciate adequately the experience by examining its consequences only from the perspective of individuals. The movement of which it is a part must also be examined.

2. The Social Aspect of the Spirit's Work

Interior workings of the Spirit do not occur in a void. They happen to individuals who are shaped to a greater or lesser extent by their culture. The form they take, as we have intimated, is influenced to some degree by the needs and values of the world around them. To adequately grasp this insight, however, it is necessary to see God's work in a broader perspective. His plan, as Vatican II has told us, is to call a people together. He works in the midst of historical forces and events. It is not necessary to turn to ancient history for examples such as Cyrus or even Augustine's analysis of Rome and its fall to understand their relationship. Although those concerned with the scientific study of history have shied away from such interpretations, it is possible to see God's hand in recent events as well.[3] The relationship between Napoleon and the papacy is an interesting case in point. Although there are many factors at work in Napoleon's fall, there is a deeper force. The remarkable story of his relations with the Church and his designs for the papacy bear this out. He had intended to deal with his prisoner, Pope Pius VII, upon his return from the Russian campaign. The famous retreat from Moscow needs no retelling. It ended his designs.[4] It is not our purpose here to indulge in such theorizing. I advance this speculation merely to state that even though it be difficult to discern at any given point, there can be no doubt for a Christian that God acts in history.

In carrying out his plans, he has used a variety of instruments. His principal vehicle of grace, the Church, is not so much our concern at this point. Rather, we will focus our attention on the less enduring phenomenon by which both the Church and society are influenced and moved. Most people have encountered examples of these instruments. They are centers of influence for others, drawing them to a deeper love of Christ and a fuller life of service. For instance, an individual—priest, nun or lay person—who exerts a positive influence over a group of people is such an instrument. The size or extent of influence can vary from a few people to large masses, and time periods extend from a span of several years to many generations. Seen in this perspective, the world is full of thousands of centers of Christian influence. Each, in varying degrees, is a tool or instrument which the Spirit can use to influence, help, or encourage men. Such centers commonly are based upon a dynamic individual, a method, or a subject of concern. Some are movements in the sense that a deliberate effort is made to spread knowledge and to involve others; many are not. Some are organized in the sense that a division of responsibilities toward the accomplishment of tasks exists. Some have evolved into institutions through which a way of life has been forged in order to facilitate and strengthen the insight or goal. It is often the case that a given instrument will demonstrate many of these features. For example, the fine work of Billy Graham is built upon his wonderful gifts, influences masses, and is organized. The ministry of a parish priest who does good for many souls, based upon his love and gifts, may not be organized and will reach fewer people. To some extent, he will utilize the methodology of the Church—e.g., confession, matrimony, catechism, etc.—to influence people. The rosary crusade of Fr. Peyton is built around a man and a method—saying the rosary. It is also a movement. The cursillo is also a movement built upon a method, the cursillo weekend and the group reunion and weekly gathering of cursillistos. The Christian Family Movement and the liturgical movements focus upon areas of the life of God's people. Frequently, a successful movement will develop a methodology and an organization and give rise to institutions. The Franciscan movement centered around the person of St. Francis and developed into institutions affecting many generations in the families of Franciscan religious orders. The work of St. Ignatius, dependent of course on his personality, also developed a method in the Exercises which also became an independent source of influence for many, particularly through his founding of the Jesuit order.

The scope and influence of these tools are affected, and to some degree evoked, by a variety of factors. Two forces warrant attention. The first involves the events and circumstances of the times. The need for a movement of renewal, the rise of cities and the mercantile classes, and the sad state of many clerics set the stage for the Franciscan renewal. Unlike the great orders that had served the Church through monasteries or settled holdings, the Franciscans were to be mendicant, going from town to town and living with the people. Both in style and approach, this movement met a need of the times and to a considerable extent renewed the Church in the 12th century. In an earlier age which was more agrarian and settled, the monastic movement met the needs of the age in a different manner. Today, the disintegration of social institutions, even the family, and the increasing secularization of society form the background for any religious movement. To be successful, a movement must meet the needs of the times. A second force is the loyalty of those whom the Lord calls to serve him through these centers of influence. If these movements are genuine, they proceed not from a good idea but a longing, a love which God places in some men's hearts. Usually the process by which the longing is worked out requires much time and suffering. The loyalty of men to God's call is a factor as real, if not as tangible, as the external circumstances of the age. In every age, God has chosen to act through men as his instruments. A Moses, David, St. Francis, or St. Ignatius, to name only a few, played an integral role in his plans at strategic moments in history. Had they not responded so generously, history would have been different. These men and many who joined them were faced with a choice and opened their hearts to the love which God placed there.

With these two forces in mind, we can begin to see the place of spiritual movements. They are intermediate or short-range tools by which God can facilitate transitions or accommodate specific needs or enable his people to grow. They will not endure as will the Church. They are, in fact, only fruitful insofar as they are ordered to the Church. Nonetheless, they are an important aspect of God's work. It must also be noted that at any given point there always seem to be a variety of such movements which have the potential to benefit the Christian people. Some affect large portions of the people of God; others do not. Some have stressed certain elements which called for emphasis at a given time; others have stressed different elements. For example, the Franciscan and Jesuit movements were different. Each was effective, the genius of each meeting a particular need of the Church. One special benefit of such movements is that they offer a valuable tool to increase and deepen the fervor of Christians and a force to attract others to Christ. Quite frequently they offer an opportunity for an experience or encounter with Christ to the individual which generates the spiritual awakening of which we have spoken previously. As such, they play a valuable role in God's work. The result of such experiences frequently is a deep transformation and release by which tremendous psychic energies are released. There is no era in the history of the Christian people in which these movements did not have a role. Their function is supplementary to the established life of the Church. This dimension of God's work is far more valuable than the movements of which we have been speaking, were the two to be compared. In reality, it is foolish to do so, for they complement each other. Indeed, it is an inevitable dynamic of successful spiritual movements that they seek to create tools in which the experience can be lived out, and so become established in their own turn. The regular and ordinary life of the Church is where the deepest work of grace takes place. Spiritual movements come and go; the Church abides.

Throughout the history of Christianity such movements have been regarded with a certain ambivalence, and with good reason. They have often been sources of disruption and dissension. Some have done harm to their members. At times, they have posed a threat to Church leaders. They have been a mixed blessing. More often than may be recognized, I believe, the fault lies in the inability of Church leaders to see the need of such movements for their leadership and formation. Often the externals of such movements are repulsive, but underneath are hearts yearning for Christ. When this has been recognized, the fruits have been tremendous. Although St. Francis is often applauded for his loyalty to God, there may be insufficient recognition of the wisdom of Pope Innocent III in tapping this source of energy for the Church and in guiding it, for it was not without its dangers. It must, however, be recognized as well that often the narrow-mindedness and pride of would-be agents whom God wishes to use prevent a movement from being fully effective.

Where a mysterious mixture of forces and factors have combined to produce an authentic spiritual movement, there has been a work of grace. Men have been freed, opened to a life of charity, and drawn into the bosom of the Church. There, the life of an age has been influenced and modified to some extent. There, the Kingdom has been tasted, if only in a fleeting way.

It is in this social context, then, that the work of God in the life of an individual must be viewed. The experience at the heart of the charismatic renewal cannot be adequately understood unless it is seen in the context of an historical spiritual movement. Only time will tell if the charismatic movement is to have a serious impact on the life of the Church. There are some indications that it may. The charismatic experience of the Spirit is received in the context of this movement, and those who receive are influenced not only by this experience but by the movement as well. In its Life in the Spirit seminars and prayer meetings, it has a methodology and also organizations of sorts to promote it and has given rise in some prayer groups to nascent institutions.

C. An Explanation of the Charismatic Experience of the Holy Spirit

The charismatic experience can best be understood in reference to two inter-related features. (1) It is a source of spiritual growth for an individual. (2) It is at the center of a spiritual movement.

The experience is intimately related to the charismatic renewal. The sense in which we speak of movement is not so much in its sociological dimensions as in its spiritual dimensions. That is, the renewal is conceived of as a work of God's Spirit in response to a unique historical, social, and political situation. It is a movement addressed to the needs of the times. It has the potential of working a deep renewal of the Church. The charismatic experience is a means of drawing men into this movement. In this sense it represents a call to love the Church in a certain way, out of a certain framework with given ideals and emphases. Despite enormous differences, charismatics are united by common desires and common expressions of response to God. By yielding to the graces of the charismatic experience, an individual opens himself as well to the particular graces of a proclivity for community, exercise of the charisms, and sensitivity to the charismatic leadings of the Spirit— to name but a few. Although the common spirituality and emphases of charismatics can be analyzed in sociological terms, these features result not from a common ideology but from a grace common to the initial experience. The charismatic experience, in short, is ordered to a particular work of grace with specific dimensions.

It is also an experience which intensifies or accelerates an individual's spiritual life. The effect of the experience depends, quite naturally, upon the individual's state of growth. The charismatic experience affects the spiritually dead and it affects those who are spiritually mature. Its influence corresponds to the needs and situation of the individual receiving it. It gives life to those who are dead, awakens those who slumber, advances those who have begun, deepens those who are advanced. For many it will serve as part of the process of initiation and conversion, serving as one particular experience of the Holy Spirit. For others who have already had an experience of the Holy Spirit, it will be accompanied by necessary graces for particular needs.

The charismatic experience, then, is a particular grace, marked by its own unique features or characteristics, which accelerates the spiritual life of an individual. It is distinct from other graces, given by God throughout the history of the Church and at the present time, which are marked by different features and addressed to different needs. Nonetheless, it is in its essence but another manifestation of the work of the same Spirit whose end remains constant but who ceaselessly works new wonders by which to renew the face of the earth.

A consequence of this conceptual approach to the charismatic experience is that the experience and movement are seen as one way of many that God has worked to renew his Church. Two points must be noted in this regard.

1. The tendency toward elitism must be avoided in all its forms. For anyone who has been opened to the realities of the spiritual life and the presence of the Spirit, it is obvious that all who do not have such an openness and awareness are missing something important. It is not, however, wise or correct to judge an individual's awareness of the Spirit by the channel through which he works. Because of the social and historical dimensions of movements of grace, the marks or features which accompany the spiritual experience differ. Comparisons are difficult and hazardous because the needs which God addresses differ and because any given individual may well find different levels of needs met through different movements of grace. Indeed, it is true that for some individuals other movements were merely preparatory compared to the work of grace in the charismatic renewal. On the other hand, there are numerous situations in which the charismatic renewal served a preparatory purpose in an individual's life. To simply judge an experiential awareness of the Spirit on the basis of the graces particular to the charismatic renewal is a mistake. It is not the only or most important way God has chosen to work among all men. It is one way—and for some, it seems, the most important. There have been and are, however, other deep works of grace with different features which cannot be ignored. To name but one, the Little Brothers and Sisters of Jesus represent a much more quiet and hidden movement of grace. The depth and power of this work cannot be doubted. The "size" of its impact cannot truly be measured, either, by quantity. What matters is the loyalty of those called through this work of grace to God's call to them. Other works of grace, then, deserve respect and love. Those called through them must not be regarded by charismatics as benighted or spiritually immature. Some may be. Some may be drawn to a deeper work of grace. But others will have already enjoyed deeper graces, and some charismatics will be drawn to them through other movements. The wonderful successes of the renewal may increase the temptation to such an attitude of superiority. In the face of

this, a healthy humility should be cultivated. Each individual should be encouraged to be loyal to the lights given by God to him. Charismatics must not judge others by their own lights and should avoid any temptations to do so.

2. These reflections should in no way diminish a balanced and healthy enthusiasm for the charismatic renewal and experience. For those called or influenced through it, it is a way of salvation. God does not reach every individual through every movement of grace. Some people are drawn through some channels and others through others. It is, of course, necessary to keep these channels in a proper perspective. They do not, as we have indicated, replace the Church or usurp other means or works of grace. A distinction must be drawn, however, between a recognition of the channel and the response to God through it. Whatever means of grace he uses, God invites a radical and complete response. His invitation must not be met by qualifications or reservations. It must be seen as a lover's advance and responded to with a swift and joyful heart. The concrete expressions which this response will take, of course, are governed by the external features of the particular movement of grace through which he works. As a result, an individual must regard these means with appropriate loyalty and respect. It is necessary to maintain the proper interior stance of faith and love toward them. They are the ways God has chosen to work. Doubt or cynicism with regard to them should be swept aside, and faith in them should be cultivated. Charismatics, while realizing that God calls others in many ways, should also realize that he has called them in this way. This renewal and the charismatic experience of the Spirit are to be treasured in their hearts. God's ways are such that he is never far from the tool or agency he uses. What is involved, ultimately, is an expression of love. It is inconceivable that a lover would express his love through anything that he did not regard as precious. It is, then, an impossible contradiction to be drawn to God through the graces of the renewal and yet to foster a disbelief in it. Such a contradiction complicates a response which must be simple. The simple, spontaneous movement of the heart toward God is only facilitated when the channel used is itself one of wonder and awe. These reflections do not advocate a mindless approach to the renewal or an uncritical acceptance of its forms. It

does imply that such criticisms for a charismatic can only be fruitful if they proceed in and from a deep-seated love for the movement. If God has placed such a love in a person's heart, it should be cultivated and nourished, for it is a wonderful gift to be highly treasured.

An inescapable conclusion of our analysis of the charismatic experience is that it does not mark the completion of God's work in the life of a person. Treated by itself, it is incomplete. It is ordered to growth. It is, I believe, in the ability of charismatics to recognize the incompleteness of the experience and to respond to its inherent demand for growth that the impact of the charismatic movement will be determined. If the fundamental attitude of charismatics is to regard the charismatic experience as the ultimate peak of the spiritual life or to create a cult of experience, then the ability of the movement to meet the needs of the Christian people will be limited. If, on the other hand, it is recognized not as an end but as a source of tremendous energies which must be tapped, directed, and utilized toward a deeper life of charity, then it will truly be a fruitful and blessed source of renewal for all Christians.

Such a recognition is evidenced, in the first place, by the orientation of new charismatics, not so much toward a unique experience, but toward living a full Christian life. If the renewal is to bear lasting fruit, it is not enough to pray with others for the charismatic experience. If they have not been exposed to other essential elements, they must be. For example, a charismatic experience of the Holy Spirit will be of less impact where one does not have a personal relationship with Christ, has not made an act of faith in him, has not repented, or has not been baptized. Unlikely as it may seem at first, many who seek this experience and receive it have not been exposed to these other essential elements. They need such exposure if they are to grow properly. For example, if a person has not made a personal choice to serve Christ wholeheartedly, the power of the charismatic experience will soon be dissipated and he will once again be assailed by doubts and misgivings. Or if a person has not heard the Gospel, the effects of the experience will be less powerful than if he had.

Secondly, the graces of this experience must be understood as an invitation to a way of life. Having been touched by the living

Spirit of God, a person is faced with a decision. God is calling such a person to live out a life of commitment and service on even deeper levels. Charismatics must emphasize this aspect of the experience. If the charismatic experience is an isolated event, having no lasting effect on one's life, it will soon wear off as a spiritual force. To the extent to which one cooperates with God in forging a new life style in light of his grace and presence, to that extent will he be living out the experience. The nature of these changes will vary from person to person and situation to situation. It is dangerous, in fact, to propose general rules. It is often the case that this experience draws charismatics into a series of relationships with other charismatics. This social dimension of the experience is healthy and to be warmly encouraged. In this context, not only is a person's response worked out, but a pattern of relationships as well.

It must also be recognized that the essence of this experience is not emotional. Emotions are an important part of man and will necessarily be touched by any genuine experience. Especially where a person has been heavily burdened with stress or anxiety, there will often be a great emotional release accompanying the charismatic experience. When this positive feeling lessens or is absent, however, the effect of the experience has not diminished. The experience is much deeper than its emotional aspect. Doubts and darkness are to be expected, but it is possible to maintain and cultivate a living faith in God's work through this experience, and, through it, a living faith in him.

It is the purpose of this book to offer charismatics recently drawn into the movement and having received the charismatic experience some basic guidelines in five areas which deserve special attention. The effects of the charismatic experience itself and the nature of the movement are such that these areas are of great importance. It is essential that charismatics have a solid spiritual and intellectual foundation in regard to them. The areas are: the need for an authentic charismatic spirituality, building an interior life, guidance, the charismatic gifts, and charismatic community. It must be apparent that each of these areas differs. The need for an authentic charismatic spirituality and some elements of such a spirituality is addressed not only to individuals but to groups and the movement as a whole. The examination of prayer and the other essentials of the spiritual life is very basic and not particularly charismatic. It contains material which many will be familiar with but which is contained here because every new charismatic should be aware of it. Guidance and the gifts are especially influenced by the practice and discoveries of the renewal. The chapter on charismatic community examines one particular thrust of the experience and an important dimension of the movement. It is to these areas that charismatics must attend if they wish to rest their experience upon an adequate basis.

II
An Authentic
Charismatic Spirituality

For most people, religion is simply not exciting. It offers none of the attractions which appeal to the ordinary "man in the pew." Even St. Augustine lamented that many in his congregation preferred the games to the Christian assembly. Even less appealing than religion in general is spirituality in particular. It is no secret that there is much apathy among Christians—good and upright people—to the things of the Spirit. We have spoken before of a state of spiritual awareness or consciousness. One who is spiritually awake finds religion to be a source of life and power. Such a person is highly motivated and often anxious for guidance and formation. In the general scheme of things such a person stands out.

Charismatics have been so awakened. The effect of the charismatic experience on most people who receive it is to bring to life or reawaken a lively spiritual sensitivity and to stimulate a spiritual hunger. Instead of the usual indifference with which most people respond to the spiritual realm, charismatics respond with an eagerness and sense of urgency which is sometimes alarming. At times it turns individuals who could hardly have been dragged into a church at Christmas into fanatics pounding down the church door. What happens, of course, is that in receiving this gift of the Spirit, an individual is attracted by a whole dimension of reality of which previously he may have been hardly aware.

Popular thought has either dismissed or diminished the spiritual as a force in life, seeing it as an escape for eccentrics. Men of past ages were more aware of it than men today. They took the spiritual very seriously, albeit oftentimes through warped and crude means such as demon worship, magic or spells. Modern man is not totally unaware of the reality of the spiritual world. In the enlightened and civilized world, however, the popular mind, having on the whole rejected the importance of the spiritual for a closed and limited universe, has placed its faith in science and progress. It has swept under the rug any possibility of the existence of a spiritual dimension of reality not defined by and ordered to the world which men see and hear.

Predictably, it leaves a big lump in the rug. Man, however much he may deny it, is not only a material being, ensconced in the here and now universe. He is a spiritual being as well, and he has a capacity—one might even say a yearning—for the spiritual. This hunger for things of the spirit has surfaced in almost all of man's endeavors and marked those which were most noble. Through it men of every age have found peace and happiness. Furthermore, the spiritual order exists as a real force affecting human affairs. It is something which men almost instinctively look for, and only by the recognition of it can reality be satisfactorily explained.

Through the charismatic experience, the spiritual realm becomes immediate and real, and religion assumes a freshness which may have never before been present or else may have been absent for some time. It could be said that a sixth sense—a spiritual one—was awakened by the charismatic experience by which men can "sense" or "see" an aspect of reality not before perceived. Through the charismatic experience, there is a sudden awareness of and attraction toward the reality of God, the power and joy of his presence, and the fulfillment that can be found in loving him and serving him. These truths may have been accepted and acted upon previously, but they take on a new inner force as a result of this experience.

There is, of course, in this experience occasion for bewilderment, discouragement, and even despair. Without the benefit of years of serious Christian formation, a charismatic could well be adrift. New charismatics need an adequate understanding of the things of the Spirit and an adequate program of spirituality. Without such an understanding and program, there is much less likelihood that the charismatic experience will come to fruition. The charismatic renewal opens the possibility of a new way of life lived out at a deeper level. The purpose of the Spirit's work is to transform and sanctify men. If this is to happen, though, the initial act of explicitly and deliberately opening oneself to the Spirit's work must be followed up by an ever deepening openness and surrender. It must be remembered, though, that the experience does not take place in a void but in the context of a spiritual movement. As a result, the explanation and program available to most new charismatics is that of the charismatic renewal. The renewal offers them a spirituality, that is, a system of piety supported by a theoretical approach to Christianity.

The spirituality through which the experience is lived out is of the greatest consequence. A rich spirituality offers a deliberate approach to life by which one seeks to cooperate totally with the sanctifying work of the Holy Spirit. In the normal affairs of life it is easy to be misled and confused unless goals are unmistakably set out. The same principle applies to the spiritual order. Any infirmity of resolution to pursue sanctification is remedied by an explicit and articulated statement of a goal and the program by which it is to be achieved. Such a method or discipline enables a person to maintain fervor and focus upon a goal in the face of distractions or difficulties. The need for such an approach to the serious matters of life is widely recognized. For instance, in the world of business, management experts have created an entire type of literature advising how to attain goals, or, better put, how to live a good and happy life—for this is the scope of their endeavor. For the Christian a spirituality serves this purpose. It is not a luxury but a necessity. Long before the modern world sought to understand and articulate the means by which goals are achieved, saints had worked out serious and total approaches to life and initiated others into them. Such approaches have focused not only upon the things of the Spirit, but have encompassed every aspect of life, and properly so, for the spiritual dimension of a man is not an abstraction but part of the whole man. A spirituality, therefore, must immerse itself in the things of earth in order to find, as it were, the raw material for the new heavenly man. There is a special need for a spirituality in the modern world if one is to grow spiritually. There exist today not only competing ideologies which seek to provide a total way of life for man, such as communism, facism, and satanism, but also a broadly based materialism which has penetrated East and West and has dulled modern man and fed him an ideology based on the equation of consumption and happiness. A vital Christian spirituality is necessary in the face of these forces.

As a Christian movement in the modern world, the charismatic renewal must offer its adherents a spirituality of sufficient vitality and depth. The graces of the Spirit's work are available not only in the charismatic experience itself but available to individuals and the movement as a whole to create an adequate spirituality. If the full work of renewal and transformation which the Spirit wishes to accomplish is to be completed, the response of charismatics to these graces must be at least as full and enthusiastic as is their response to the charismatic experience. Through such a response, they will develop an authentic spirituality appropriate to this movement of grace.

The essential characteristics of an authentic spirituality can be identified.

1. It must be *contemporary*.
2. It must be *catholic*.
3. It must be *charismatic*.

Let us examine these characteristics.

1. *It Must Be Contemporary*

An authentic charismatic spirituality must be in tune with what God is saying to the world today. It must be sensitive to the needs and aspirations of modern times. Suggesting that an authentic spirituality must be contemporary, however, is not saying necessarily that it should be popular. In every age, some aspects of the Gospel will be acceptable to men in general. It is the aspect of the Gospel which is rejected or ignored in any given age that an authentic spirituality must bring to the attention of men. It has a prophetic role of proclaiming the fullness of Christ's Gospel and of emphasizing those aspects of the Gospel which, in God's eyes, the world most needs to hear. It must also seek to relate to and support the authentic aspirations of men in a given age for what is good and true. These aspirations are also works of the Spirit, and it is the responsibility of an authentic spirituality to cooperate with all men of good will in such aspirations. An authentic spirituality must, as it were, forge a way of life in which the full Gospel is lived out as an effective witness to the world. In our time, for example, an authentic spirituality must seek to sustain and promote the family as the nuclear unit for social order. It must seek to foster a deep reverence for life, especially among the poor, aged, and unborn. It must sustain a lively sense of social justice. And it must seek to foster community among men.

2. *It Must Be Catholic*

An authentic spirituality must be deeply rooted in a charismatic's Christian heritage. A movement of the Spirit seeks to renew in a way which builds upon whatever is good and authentic. Human renewal is more often the sort which must demolish and obliterate and start anew. The Spirit, however, continually works to deepen, transform, and renew in a wondrous manner that draws upon past riches to provide new patterns of love and worship. Each charismatic must allow the Spirit to reveal the riches of his tradition and to work his marvels through these channels of grace. Rather than rudely uprooting tradition, an authentic spirituality is a true continuation of it in a given age. Charismatics must see themselves in a long line of believers stretching back to the apostles and Christ and respect this channel of grace in which they have been formed. Indeed, an authentic spirituality calls for much more than a political adherence to Church; it requires a deep loyalty on the part of a Christian to the tradition in which he has been nourished. Of course, there will be a need to distinguish between vessels of grace suited for a particular age or need and those of lasting or universal value. Such a process, though, is crucial if the spirituality which emerges from the renewal is to have deep roots.

For example, for Roman Catholics an authentic spirituality must be founded on the revelation of Christ living in the Church which is its authentic interpreter. It must be nourished by God's Word in Scripture and the teachings of the Church. It must be deeply sacramental and its prayer life must be centered upon the public prayer of the Church, especially the Mass. Its teachings should be shaped in reference to the great spiritualities which God has raised up in the Church and the great doctors of the Church whose teaching and example provide a rich heritage. It must also sustain an active faith in the pastors of the Church, obeying them and seeking from them counsel and direction. An authentic spirituality which is Catholic must actively cultivate its catholicity and work to forge deep bonds of unity with the Church.

For charismatics of other denominations, a similar principle must be applied. The spirituality of the renewal, to be authentic, must be rooted in a reverence for the tradition in which God has worked to form them.

Founded on a healthy respect for the means in which God's grace has worked, it is then possible to cultivate a respect for other traditions and to rejoice in the common basis which Scripture, a common love of Christ, and the experience of the Spirit provide. In this sense, an authentic spirituality must have a broad respect and love for the integrity of every genuine work of grace while maintaining an ever present loyalty to the lights offered by God through a given tradition.

3. *It Must Be Charismatic*

An authentic spiritual movement must be loyal to its nature. Through this movement, the Spirit obviously wishes to witness to the power of God in a dramatic manner. Certainly these charismatic workings must be kept in a balanced perspective. Without charity, they are empty; without order, they do not edify. We will discuss these matters at length in Chapter 4. It is the charismatic himself who first of all should be poignantly aware of the limitations of the gifts. Yet with all of these qualifications in mind, the charismatic must never be ashamed of this feature of the Lord's work. The Church also needs a charismatic witness, especially in these days. Charismatics must boldly strive to be faithful ministers of the charismatic gifts, using them with integrity and dignity for the upbuilding and benefit of the whole Church. Not only in reference to the specific charismatic gifts, however, is the charismatic quality of the renewal to be understood. The renewal also signifies the need and opportunity for men to cultivate an inner sensitivity to the leadings of the Spirit and to strive to be loyal to them. In this sense, too, the charismatic, led by the Spirit, must witness in accord with the particular graces of this movement. The insight into and recognition of the charismatic dimension must be translated by new charismatics into a feature of their regular pattern of life. Indeed, for all charismatics, this dimension must be a healthy and full aspect of their spirituality if they are to be true to the inspirations of the Spirit. To paraphrase St. Paul, they must not "despise prophecy, nor quench the Spirit, but test all things, holding fast what is good and abstaining from what is bad" (1 Thes. 5:19-22).

As a charismatic reflects upon his experience and incorporates it into his life, his spirituality develops. A broader charismatic spirituality is unfolding as well in various prayer groups and throughout the movement as a whole; it evolves through a combination of practice and teaching. As it unfolds, it is necessary for individual, group, and movement to test it and shape it in idea and practice to insure its soundness and authenticity. Every enthusiastic movement encounters stumbling blocks and is in danger of losing either sanity or sanctity. The charismatic renewal is no exception. The remainder of this chapter will treat several important considerations for new charismatics in formulating an authentic charismatic spirituality.

Some Considerations Regarding
an Authentic Charismatic Spirituality

1. The Call to Holiness

An authentic spirituality must have as its aim an uncompromising quest for holiness. Holiness must be, in a sense, the goal that shapes and determines all other interests. Holiness, of course, is not something that men can attain unaided. God alone is holy, and to become holy is to share in God's holiness. Holiness does not come primarily from ritual actions, pious practices, self-confidence, or works. Its source is Christ, and a person is sanctified by a participation in Christ's saving work. On another level, however, this work involves a full and active cooperation on our part. God expects and invites an ongoing personal consecration by which every thought, action, value, and even the most intimate movements of mind and heart are ordered in love to him.

Jesus called his disciples to total consecration. He said:

"If anyone comes to me and does not hate his own father and mother and wife and children and brothers and sisters, yes, and even his own life, he cannot be my disciple. Whoever does not bear his own cross and come after me cannot be my disciple. For which of you, desiring to build a tower, does not first sit down and count the cost, whether he has enough to complete it? Otherwise, when he has laid a foundation, and is not able to finish, all who see it begin to mock him, saying, 'This man began to build, and was not able to finish.' Or what king, going to encounter another king in war, will not sit down first and take counsel whether he is able with ten thousand to meet him who comes against him with twenty thousand? And if not, while the other is yet a great way off, he sends an embassy and asks terms of peace. So, therefore, whoever of you does not renounce all that he has cannot be my disciple" (Lk. 14:26-33).

It is clear in his teaching that following him took priority over even the closest relationships between parents, and husband and wife. So that no one could mistake his meaning, Jesus uses the verb "hate" to mark the contrast in a disciple's attitude between even these cherished relationships and devotion to him. Christ calls for loyalty even in the face of the most brutal of executions. To reinforce this point, he cites two stories (Lk. 14:28-32). Both point to those who began something without counting the cost and were unable to complete what they had begun. The implication is that at the outset of living the Christian life it is wise to consider the cost, so as to be prepared to pay it. Christ takes great pains in this text and elsewhere to make it clear that the "cost" is everything: "Whoever of you does not renounce all that he has cannot be my disciple" (Lk. 14:33). The lesson here is obvious for those charismatics beginning a serious Christian life. St. Paul writes: "This is the will of God, your sanctification" (1 Thes. 4:3). Recalling the language of the Pentateuch, the author of 1 Peter admonishes: "As he who called you is holy, be holy yourselves in all your conduct, since it is written, 'You shall be holy, for I am holy' " (1 Pt. 1:16). Christ shuns any compromise in his call: "No one can serve two masters; for either he will hate the one and love the other, or he will be devoted to the one and despise the other. You cannot serve God and mammon" (Mt. 6:24). All Christian teaching on perfection is summarized, though, in this command: "You, therefore, must be perfect, as your heavenly Father is perfect" (Mt. 5:48).

The Christian life is ordered to holiness, and the vocation of a Christian is particularly a call to perfection. The Christian is made holy by Christ. He is a member of a holy people, a people set apart for the service and praise of God. Personally, he must seek to put on this holiness in every aspect of his being and character. Any authentic spirituality must make perfection its goal. A charismatic, therefore, must aim at perfection; nothing less will do. It is not sufficient for charismatics to be pious or to take as their standard common religious practice by which they may appear to excel. Their standard must be Christ and they must strive to imitate him.

2. Some Objections

There are, of course, many objections to a view of Christianity which emphasizes the call to total consecration to God. Aside from the indifference of the world, many Christians themselves reject such a notion as fanatical or extreme. There are, indeed, ways of living Christianity which are fanatical or extreme in a bad sense. At its essence, though, it is Christianity itself which is extreme. Christ warned that the world would love its own and hate those who were not its own (Jn. 15:18-25). Such a warning is still apt today. There will always be some aspect of Christianity which is too much for any era or time. Today, the left commends and endorses Christian social teaching while passing over in silence subjects like prayer, fasting, celibacy, the interior life, and devotion to God. The right sees an intense piety as a bulwark for what it believes good but becomes suspicious when the love of neighbor is taken "too far," especially in its social, political or economic implications. The Christian, combining an effective compassion with an intense piety, must always be an enigma to the men of any age.

There also exists a deep-seated notion among Catholics that religion in an all-embracing sense is the business of the "religious." There is a tendency in Catholic teaching and practice which has reinforced this distorted spiritual teaching. Fortunately, the Second Vatican Council has forthrightly stated what is the correct understanding of Christ's teaching. It declares: "Fortified by so many and such powerful means of salvation, all the faithful, whatever their condition or state, are called by the Lord, each in his own way, to that perfect holiness whereby the Father himself is perfect" (*Constitution on the Church*, n. 11). These objections are often rooted in an unwillingness to surrender one's life totally to God. A life in which some Christian ideals are important but which is not ordered to God in a radical way is incomplete. Jesus came into the world to inaugurate a deeper relationship between God and man.

3. The World

Another barrier to an authentic spirituality consists in the popular image of the "holy" or devout individual. In a caricature, such a person lives a miserable, other-worldly life of penance and austerity. The popular mind rejects such an image. It must be conceded that there is much about it to be rejected. A regrettable tendency in Christian spirituality which fosters a false attitude toward the things of creation has cropped up from time to time. Its result has been a narrowness and stiffness with regard to what is in itself good and holy—one which more resembles the attitude and behavior of a Manichaean than of Jesus. This tendency has been soundly rejected by the Church. It is, in fact, often the very saints such as Augustine or Bernard who themselves practiced an intense devotional life who were most outspoken in their rejection of this error. Despite the balance which Catholic spirituality has sought to maintain, there is a strong identification in the popular mind between this tendency and a wholesome Christian spirituality. Because of their inexperience, many new charismatics are subject to this tendency—seeing everything through ultra-spiritual other-worldly glasses.

Scripture offers a valuable insight into this area. God created everything and found all that he created to be good (Gn. 1:31). Any spirituality which does not rejoice in the goodness of creation is stunted. Jesus himself took pleasure in what was good, true, and beautiful, as did those men and women who have imitated him so closely. Any adequate treatment of the life of a saint will reveal, above all, one who is bluntly—almost starkly—human. But there is more to be said here. It must also be recognized that God loved this world, stains and all. Jesus gave his life for it (Jn. 3:16). St. Paul says that all of creation groans in travail, awaiting the revealing of the sons of God (Rom. 8:19-20). This world, then, which is the object of God's love, is not something a Christian can despise.

However, it would be foolish to conclude from these reflections that the Christian can naively embrace the world and immerse himself in it. Such foolishness has affected many Christians and especially some Christian teachers today. The world will not now willingly hear the good news or endure its proclamation any more than it ever has. Christians can expect at its hands the same treatment which Christ received. After Vatican Council II there were those who, discovering for themselves the good of creation, became intoxicated by the world. Scripture speaks of the world not only as God's creation, but as in bondage to sin and ruled by the prince of darkness who is called the ruler of the world (Jn. 12:31; 14:30; 16:11). Any notion of the world which fails to recognize this ambiguity and confuses God's love with an undiscriminating endorsement of the world cannot be faithful to Christ.

The seed of truth in the popular caricature of the Christian "saint" is that, in the end, the Christian does "reject" the world. His rejection, though, is not stoic, nor does it stem from some desire for self-punishment. It is the choice of something better. Understood from an exterior vantage point, especially that of the sensual, such a course is negative and perverse. Understood in its true perspective, though, the saint chooses the better portion. In describing the difference or seeking to reinforce fervor, the world and the things of the world are sometimes treated by the saint with contempt. It must be realized that the love which so ardently embraces the life of perfection, if it is genuine, also ardently and humbly takes pleasure in all that is good, true, and right (Phil. 4:8).

The contempt of the saint is not for the world as such but as an obstacle to the love of God. To be in the world but not of the world is
no easy matter (Jn. 17:14-16). An authentic spirituality, however,
will seek to maintain this tension between the love and denial of
the world if it is in imitation of Christ.

4. The New Man

Perfection involves putting on a new nature (Col. 3:10; Eph.
4:22-24). "Putting on Christ," being "born anew" (Jn. 3:3; 1 Pt.
1:23), and having "died" (Col. 2:12) are the terms used in Scripture to describe the transformation that takes place when one
becomes a Christian. St. Paul writes: "If anyone is in Christ, he is
a new creation; the old has passed away, behold, the new has
come" (2 Cor. 5:17).

The new charismatic must also be transformed. He must
strive to grow in the new nature, to put on the new man. Transformation in Christ does not occur in one experience. It means
change. The extent to which an individual must change depends, of
course, on the state of his relationship with God and, to some
degree, the extent of his Christian formation.

Involvement in the charismatic renewal itself usually brings
with it some changes. Not all of them are of equal value, however.
In fact, at times some changes can be deceptive because they give
the illusion of important change when in reality they are super-
ficial. To compare them, we will examine some changes which
charismatics undergo: change of mannerism, change of behavior,
change of thought, and change of attitude.

Change of mannerism occurs most commonly. Charismatics
behave differently from others in a variety of ways. It is normal
for a person becoming involved in the renewal to adopt charismatic mannerisms—often without thinking about it. Two examples
will illustrate this point. Charismatics commonly embrace one another. This gesture is awkward and cumbersome for most non-
charismatics. After a time of sharing in similar experiences and
fellowship, it comes easily to new charismatics. The expression
"Praise the Lord!" is also commonly used among charismatics. To
outsiders, it is jarring. A new person comes to use it almost with-

out a thought after a rather short time. These changes represent an important type of change. They signify that an individual is identifying with a group and picking up its behavior and values. Where these patterns of behavior and values are good, this step is a positive one. It is not, however, the most important change which a person can make. It is possible, for example, to embrace someone while harboring hatred or jealousy of him. It is also possible to exclaim "Praise the Lord!" and mean something unprintable. Change of mannerism, therefore, while good, is not the most significant type of change.

Change of thought also commonly occurs when a person becomes involved in the charismatic renewal. Patterns of thought gradually are altered and transformed and replaced by Christian patterns and values. One example would be a change in thinking about morality. Exposure to the charismatic experience may result in the adoption of a Christian approach to the moral order. As an individual receives teaching and grows in understanding of Christ's commands, inadequate or incomplete ideas about life and reality are reformed in favor of a Christian approach to reality. Another change which commonly occurs among charismatics is the development of a positive attitude toward Christian community. Frequently, individuals coming into the renewal are indifferent or hostile to the idea of community. After exposure to the charismatic dimension, they commonly begin to think of community in a positive way and adopt or develop a conceptual framework in which to understand its value and place in the Christian life. Such changes are very important. In order for an individual to completely serve God, he must do so with his mind. The intellect was made by God to embrace and love the true. The more that an individual can understand what is good and the order of things which God has established, the more completely will he be able to serve God. Change of thought, however, can be deficient too. True and proper ideas about the role of community can, for example, be used to pressure others into a course of action that they do not desire. Proper ideas about morality can also become the basis for a blind and hateful self-righteousness. Christian patterns of thought, in other words, can be ill-used to serve unchristian ends.

Change of behavior also occurs. The inner forces released by

the charismatic experience often enable a new charismatic to dis-
gard sinful or deficient patterns of behavior. The renewal is
frequently the occasion for an individual to put order into his
life and activity. For example, it can be the occasion for a parent
to put family ahead of career, recreation, or society. Such changes
are important, too, but moral behavior is not the deepest change a
Christian can make.

There is, too, a level which can be called a change of attitude. It is possible, for example, to know and do the right action in
the wrong spirit. An ordinary chore, for instance, can either be a
labor of love or not. The attitude in which daily jobs and tasks are
undertaken is significant. Even more important is the attitude with
which a person approaches his or her state in life. It is possible to
understand the Christian significance of one's state but to undertake duties and responsibilities in the wrong attitude. The tasks of
parenthood, for example, can be faced with joy and trust in God or
they can be inwardly resented and begrudgingly accomplished. The
attitude in which something is done or in which a person lives is
extremely important. A task undertaken in a Christian spirit and
the same task undertaken in the wrong spirit are two very different
tasks even though they may appear similar externally. The energies released by the charismatic experience can serve to effect interior change of heart. Without a change of attitude or change of
heart, the charismatic experience will amount to nought. It is
above all at this level that charismatics must actively work for
change.

5. Consecration to Christ

The basis of Christian perfection is total consecration of oneself to Christ. In one sense, consecration sums up Christian perfection. The person who is consecrated to God serves him totally and
exclusively. Another sense of consecration, however, focuses upon
the initial act of consecration by which a person declares his intention to be consecrated. Such a consecration is consecration by intention. By intention, a person consecrates all that he is and has to
Christ in the most explicit, solemn, and conscious manner. Such a
consecration is, of course, incomplete and needs to be followed up

by a life and life style which seeks to put the intention into effect. An act of consecration, however, is of genuine value and a real source of grace.

The initial consecration of which we speak can be confused easily with conversion, faith, and a salvation experience. The Protestant community has given this area considerable attention. The notions of conversion and a salvation experience have received only a cursory and suspicious treatment from some Catholic quarters. Although there is a commonplace reference to a "second conversion" in older Catholic literature, the terms—used frequently in the renewal—have produced some confusion. Much of the problem stems from a difference in emphasis. Concerned to preserve the efficacy of Christ's saving act and the importance of faith, some Protestants have fixed upon an act of faith as the focal point in one's struggle for salvation. Other Protestants would link this act with a salvation experience. The term "saved" is often used in regard to both emphases, thereby producing much confusion. Catholics, on the other hand, have been concerned to emphasize the ongoing work of salvation, seeing it as being completed only at the parousia and regarding any preliminary head count of the saved with chagrin. Furthermore, they have resisted, and rightly so, the implication that such an experience is the only true sign of a Christian.

Without attempting to discuss these positions in detail, let us try to sort out some practical conclusions which can be of assistance to charismatics:

● There is an experience of Christ or conversion experience. Such an experience has ample precedence in Scripture and the lives of the saints. St. Paul and St. Augustine are classic examples.

● Such an experience can occur to someone who has been baptized and who has even practiced Christianity for many years.

● Such experiences are not rare.

● They are not, necessarily, dramatic or emotional.

● They are not the measure of whether or not one is a Christian.

● They are special and privileged gifts which enable a person to focus on Christ and turn to him with concentration and fervor.

●They need to be followed up by a serious attempt to live out the Christian life.

●God does not give everyone an experience in turning to Christ.

While a conversion experience may or may not occur to a given individual, a commitment or consecration to Christ is something which every Christian seeking perfection should seriously undertake. Consecration to Christ means opening up one's life completely and totally to him. It is a conscious act or resolution, not an experience. It implies a commitment of one's personal resources to Christ in an explicit and conscious way. This commitment includes the use of time and energy, the use of free time, and the use of material resources. Today time and energy are an individual's most valuable possessions. To be seriously committed to Christ, these resources must be at his disposal. A commitment to Christ may not require a radical change in the use of time and energy. It does, however, call for a radical interior change. Jobs and duties are now done for the sake of Christ. One's time is for the service of God and his people. In this light some interruptions which would formerly have been sources of annoyance can become opportunities for service. Other people in such a light will become matters for concern and care rather than objects to be dealt with or ignored. Commitment to Christ may call for an immediate change in the way in which free time is spent. Any changes, of course, should be attended by prayer and discernment. Additional pious activities, for example, may not be in order. God may be more pleased were an individual to spend free time with the family than by any other use of it. The use of material resources, especially extra money, also is an area which commitment to Christ affects. In fact, how a person spends extra money and free time serves as a good indication of what is important in his or her life. Commitment to Christ involves making him the most important object in a person's life and reordering priorities accordingly.

A specific act of consecration is important. By explicitly and seriously committing oneself to Christ, a person provides himself with valuable psychological and spiritual support. Such a commitment is especially appropriate at major turning points in a person's life. It should be made in conjunction with receiving the charismatic experience. The preparation course commonly used for the charismatic experience encourages such a commitment, and if that commitment has not been made, it should be.

Several steps are suggested here as a pattern which one might follow:

a. *Preparation.* Some time—perhaps a week—should be spent in preparation for this special act of consecration. During this time moderate penance and much prayer are appropriate. Reception of the Eucharist frequently—or daily if possible—during this period would be helpful, as would the sacrament of penance. Meditation upon the texts in Scripture which describe the life of discipleship is also valuable.

b. *Renunciation.* It is important during this time to renounce anything contrary to the service of Christ. Patterns of behavior which are sinful should be identified and renounced and every intention made of reforming them. It is valuable to explicitly mention these forms of behavior and to seek God's forgiveness in conjunction with sacramental confession. It is also important to resolve to avoid company or patterns of speech or behavior which lead to sin.

c. *Consecration.* When a person is ready, he should place himself in an attitude of prayer. As sincerely as possible he should seek God's assistance in a solemn act of consecration. He should then call upon Jesus and offer himself to him totally and without any reservations. It is helpful to pray aloud, using one's own words at this time. A simple expression of love for Jesus and commitment to him is fine. Then these pledges made at baptism can be repeated:

Do you reject Satan?
I do.

And all his works?
I do.

And all his empty promises?
I do.

OR

Do you reject sin, so as to live in the freedom of God's children?
I do.

Do you reject the glamor of evil, and refuse to be mastered by sin?
I do.

Do you reject Satan, father of sin and prince of darkness?
I do.

Do you believe in God, the Father almighty, creator of heaven and earth?
I do.

Do you believe in Jesus Christ, his only Son, our Lord, who was born of the Virgin Mary, was crucified, died, and was buried, rose from the dead, and is now seated at the right hand of the Father?
I do.

Do you believe in the Holy Spirit, the holy catholic Church, the communion of saints, the forgiveness of sins, the resurrection of the body, and life everlasting?
I do.

God, the all-powerful Father of our Lord Jesus Christ, has given us a new birth by water and the Holy Spirit, and forgiven all our sins.
May he also keep us faithful to our Lord Jesus Christ for ever and ever.
Amen.

Finally, this prayer might be said:

Take, O Lord, and receive my entire liberty, my memory, my

understanding and my whole will. All that I am and all that I possess you have given to me. I surrender it all to you to dispose of according to your own will. Give me only your love and your grace; with these I will be rich enough and will desire nothing more.

After this act of consecration, a person should turn to God in profound thanksgiving.

Such an act of consecration is very important. An authentic spirituality is built upon total consecration to Christ. Some simple prayer of consecration, such as that suggested above, made daily, is a helpful way of fixing upon this important truth.

6. A Perspective

In seeking to lay the basis for an authentic charismatic spirituality, it helps for an individual to have a proper perspective. Any attempt to propose a general framework is obviously inadequate. Roughly speaking, though, for someone who has entered the renewal without any serious prior formation, a period of five to ten years is a reasonable time in which to lay an adequate foundation. Especially important in this regard is an adequate prayer life. Five years spent in forming deep-seated patterns of prayer would be years well spent.

Such a perspective is not given to discourage the enthusiast unnecessarily but to interject a note of realism. Unless a proper foundation is laid, anything built will not survive. A satisfactory foundation takes time to build.

The charismatic experience introduces a dynamic element into contemporary Christianity. The renewed discovery *en masse* of an experience of the Holy Spirit is something truly to be noted. Unless this experience evolves into an authentic way of life which taps the deep roots available through the Spirit's work in the Church, however, this experience and the movement which it has engendered will wither. The preliminary signs are positive. The movement is founded on a genuine spiritual awakening and has, to some degree, provided some spiritual nourishment, but the real test remains. It is yet to be seen whether charismatics can be weaned from their initial experiences and drawn to feed on the solid spiritual food which Christ has to offer them. The most important question facing this movement at this time is whether an authentic charismatic spirituality will emerge which will be catholic, contemporary, and charismatic. Put another way, the primary question facing this movement is whether it will be able to draw its masses toward a deeper interior life, abandonment of self, and total commitment to Christ. This way is by definition the narrow one. The force of the charismatic experience can be a good start. It is up to charismatics to demonstrate that the experience can be used to create men and women of deep love whose lives are shrines of grace for others. In a sense, the question is whether the movement can produce saints and a way of life which will call men to sanctity. Although an individual cannot settle this question for an entire movement, one serious decision by one person to settle for no compromise in seeking a genuine charismatic spirituality can make a powerful difference. One group whose leaders seek such a spirituality ceaselessly can influence the entire movement. The grace to so utilize the charismatic experience is there for any and all to take it. This book can and does treat some of its elements. The decision to formulate and live out such a spirituality is up to each charismatic.

III
Building an Interior Life

Christianity is, above all, a religion of the heart. It is a marriage of love between God and his people. Its meaning is summed up in God's generous and overwhelming love and his gift of his only begotten Son for the redemption of the world. Not content with these gifts, however, God has put his own Spirit of love within the heart of his people so that they might know him and love him in an intimate and personal way. The love of God is the substance of Christianity. Consequently, it is a serious business which commands the Christian's vital resources. Of all the priorities in life, it is this one which matters most. Although men do not balk at spending massive time and energy on every conceivable kind of project and enterprise, public and private, collective and individual, they are often taken aback at the suggestion of a deliberate or serious approach to the love of God. Often such a suggestion is met with the lame excuse that such things should be "spontaneous," and it is true that love in its most enjoyable and full expression cannot be planned or programed. But love, in the sense in which the word is used here, occurs in the context of an ongoing relationship. Relationships can and must be worked at if they are to bear fruit in love. Christians must work at their relationship with God, pulling weeds, as it were, watering when there is no rain, and loosening the soil if there is to be growth. This relationship must be approached with every strength and with great deliberation. It is not enough to pray, for example, when the thought occurs. It occurs far too infrequently to rely on when circumstances have a way of cluttering up each day with little things which crowd out the more important things. Any successful businessman knows the importance of putting first things first.

Above all, a living and daily relationship with God must be a

Christian's foremost goal. A living and daily relationship is one in which a person is able to spend time fruitfully in prayer each day and to sustain the grace of union with him throughout the day. Of course, every Christian is in a relationship with him throughout the day, for if no serious sin has been committed against him, or if there has been repentance for a serious sin, he is present in a privileged way. By a living and daily relationship, however, a Christian is aware of his presence and sensitive in his love for him throughout the day. Such a relationship is one in which the heart is quick to turn to him at all times and eager to please him in everything. The charismatic experience often is accompanied by a daily awareness of God. His presence fills the entire day and attracts the heart from its preoccupations to rest in him. As we have mentioned, however, this grace is often withdrawn. At such a time, it becomes imperative that new Christians begin to work to lay a foundation for a living and daily relationship. Daily spiritual exercises—however short they may be—are the principal means by which a living relationship can be nurtured. This simple truth is too often ignored by charismatics. As a result, their relationship with God has an uneven quality and is marked by an unsettling impulsiveness. There are great peaks which drop suddenly and shatteringly into abysmal pits. The value of prayer also seems to be very inconsistent. There are times of peace and fruitfulness in prayer which are separated by days or even weeks before another such period of grace. Prayer at such times seems empty and hollow. In this state patterns of growth cannot be long sustained. At times, a person may even slip back into patterns of sinful or disordered behavior.

However, the daily exercises of which we speak are not to be understood as mechanical devices practiced to attain a proficiency. They are exercises in which a Christian lifts up his heart to God. They themselves are acts of love, not simply a means, but in some sense a taste of the end as well. Because of this quality, we will use the older term "devotion" to describe them. The object of the cultivation of a life of devotion is an interior state of love which first turns to God and seeks to please him at all times and in all things. True devotion leads one to constantly abide in Christ's presence whatever the external circumstances may be.

God makes available wonderful graces to new charismatics to cultivate habits of interior devotion. By responding to them and cooperating with them, a charismatic will lay a proper foundation for a life of love. The Spirit will gently enable him or her to marshall every inner resource and to grow in interior self-discipline in a marvelous way. In this chapter we will discuss some of the ways in which charismatics can cooperate with the graces of the experience in building an interior life and cultivating true devotion. We will survey prayer (section A), Scripture (section B), the sacraments (section C), prayer with others (section D), spiritual reading (section E), and study (section F).

A. On Prayer

There is too little appreciation today of the importance of a life of prayer. Men are concerned about too many things and consequently lose or scorn the sweet recollection which Christ wishes to bring. Even among those who should know better, there is sometimes cultivated an unchristian stoic disposition which disdains the presence of the Spirit as a luxury Christians can ill afford in the face of the world's ills. Let us be frank. It is only from the deepest recollection and most sincere adoration of God that the important works needed to bring and restore a human and humane option for modern man will come. Such a work is so vast that those who would participate in it must have roots in their spirits which tap the very source of life, and they must drink deeply and regularly of it. Some may regard the expenditure of energy on an interior life as a selfish disregard of the demands of charity. On the contrary, it is the first step to a lively and effective charity. The world does not need more anxious and distressed saviors. It needs men who can put things in perspective and communicate compassion and peace. Such things can only come from one who knows peace and compassion himself. For Christians to best help the world, they must be taught these things by Christ. By drawing close to him, living in his presence, and abiding with him, they will be with Christ and able to bring him to the world. Otherwise, they will be like one who jumps in recklessly to save a drowning man only to find himself drowning too.

For the charismatic, too, there is a dynamic which de-emphasizes prayer. There is for the religious person the ever present danger of confusing the externals of godliness with an interior life and of becoming overly absorbed in the business of Christianity. With all the zeal generated by the renewal, charismatics are subject to these tendencies. Great zeal need not be either deep or wise. If professions of zeal are to lead to life, they must flow from deeply within. Indeed, the business of being a Christian, sharing the Gospel, relating with others, and seeking out community can itself usurp the central place of prayer in a relationship with God. This marriage is in this sense no different than its human counterparts; it can be one of love or it becomes cluttered by the accidents of daily living and the secondary concerns of career, outside interests, and indifference. It is within one's self that communion with God takes place and this wonderous bond of love is consummated. The charismatic who so disquiets himself even with the business of God that he cannot hear his gentle voice has cut himself off from the fullness of Christ's gift and chosen the lesser portion.

The love of God is like a delicate flower in our hearts. It is through a regular life of prayer that it is nourished and watered. It is the most precious work of the Holy Spirit through the charismatic experience to bring to life a desire for prayer where it has not been already present and to increase it where it has. Through the graces which God is making available, he is calling charismatics to a deeper pursuit of him in prayer and inviting them to an inner recollection and peace. Charismatics would do well to learn from the wise virgins to treasure and marshal the precious oil which God has poured out upon them (cf. Mt. 25:1-13). Every circumstance and every energy can be an occasion for the man or woman of prayer for an act of adoration and praise. Such an inner stance is not impossible of achievement. Indeed, the graces of the charismatic experience are a special invitation, if one is needed, to pursue such a course. A new charismatic would do well to accept it enthusiastically.

This part is not a systematic treatise on prayer. Its aim is much more modest. It is intended to touch briefly on some important considerations in building a life of prayer and to offer some general suggestions which may be helpful. It is not inspirational, but intended for those already inspired who are looking for basic guidance. In considering these suggestions, it is important to pursue only those things which are of help. There is no neat formula for building a life of prayer. It requires a normal process of trial and error as well as a serious determination. However, some program at the outset may prove of aid, and it is in this sense that the more specific suggestions are offered. Otherwise, we have tried to touch upon general principles which will be of value in forming a balanced approach to prayer. For those who have benefited from serious religious formation, such principles may appear elementary. If so, we have succeeded in our purpose.

1. Some General Reflections on Prayer

a. Its Goal

The goal of prayer is union with God. The nature of this union is most intimate and rich. Such a goal can be achieved in this life and is available to all Christians who would pursue it. This matter has long been an area of dispute among theologians, some of whom maintain that such a union is not intended by God in this life as part of the normal fare of Christians. The charismatic experience of the Holy Spirit and the renewal which it accompanies are demonstrations that special graces of prayer, while privileged, are not uncommon and that there exists in all Christians a great aptitude for the things of God. Through the charismatic experience and the renewal God has given many deep gifts of prayer and has opened many individuals to deep mystical graces. Moreover, there is a generally experienced interior sensitivity regarding the things of God. While not frequently conferring the grace of contemplative prayer through the charismatic experience, the Spirit does use it to awaken a living desire and an aptitude for it. One might call it a foretaste.

In light of this goal it can be seen that prayer, in its proper sense, is God's work. A Christian cannot place himself in union with him. There is no way that a man can so raise himself. What is commonly regarded as prayer—that is, man's effort—is only part of the picture, and not the most important part at that. Men commonly place most emphasis on their role and, so to speak, getting in their say. Thus they relegate God to a passive role. In fact, the roles should be reversed, and the objective of a person's efforts should be to seek quiet in such a way as to enable God to draw him into his presence. This notion frequently runs counter to the most common presuppositions about prayer. These presuppositions need to be carefully reviewed. If prayer is simply regarded as a one-sided activity, its most important aspect is being overlooked. By properly understanding the object of prayer, its various forms and means can be better used to quiet oneself. In a sense, a man's role is to dispose himself. Of course there will be times when it is necessary to wait without seeming to be answered. That is God's business. Our point here is that the main brunt of our efforts at prayer must be to be recollected and disposed toward God.

b. The Intellect

Another implication of this understanding of prayer is that it is not primarily a matter of the intellect. The intellect does have a role, and study is important. In prayer, though, the mind must quiet itself. It helps to feed it enough to keep its attention, but primarily to gaze, as it were, in love at God. Snatches from Scripture or the psalms can be of help in this. One should never feel as if he should be "pushing on" to absorb more intellectual content when lovingly resting in God's presence. The end of one's efforts in prayer is not intellectual achievement but loving union with God. When it is achieved, the tools must be set aside and the fruits of the labor relished.

c. Methods of Prayer

These reflections can also be of assistance in understanding the place of methods or techniques in prayer. Methods can be valuable if they quiet or dispose one toward God. They can also be distracting or become an end in themselves. Any method, however helpful, can at some point be an obstacle to union with God. There must be a basic inner freedom to set aside whatever forms or techniques have been used when God draws one to himself. There is a danger of seeking a method or technique as a "short cut" to prayer. Prayer is hard work. It requires discipline. It does not come naturally. And there is no "easy" way to prayer. There are times when prayer is easy and delightful, but these are times of grace, and these flights of spirit are due to his grace. Prayer is the most intimate expression of love for God. The attitude of prayer is that of a lover whose object is to know and to be known, to love and be loved. Anything which hinders that is bad; anything which aids it is good. We often have an acute sensitivity to those movements of spirit which more completely dispose one to God. It is important to discipline oneself to yield to him in such ways as generously and completely as possible. In its essence, that is our principal role in prayer.

d. Types of Prayer

There are various types of prayer. Petition is the type familiar to most. It is a valuable form of prayer, although not the most important. Other types of prayer should be familiar, such as contrition, thanksgiving and praise. Contrition is the state of prayer in which a person is aware of sins or sinfulness and turns to God in repentance, resolving to more fully love and serve him. Thanksgiving is not only in response to favors granted but an attitude of gratefulness for God's glory and wonder. It is the prayer of appreciation and awe at the goodness and mercy of God in all of its manifold splendor. The prayer of praise is the brightest jewel of prayer. In it, God is adored as God and worshiped. This prayer is unconcerned with needs, sins, or God's gifts and focuses on him in an act of selfless love and wonder. These distinctions shed some light on the different types of prayer. They are not, however, to be understood as steps or stages so much as movements of the heart in the act of love. A Christian goes to God in various ways in various situations. Often our prayer will contain all of these types, as, for example, does the prayer of Christians which is the Mass. It helps to understand these various types of prayer so as to be able to cooperate more consciously with God's graces and more totally enter into these states of prayer. Each of them has a place, and over a period of time it is possible to learn how to distinguish them and cooperate with them. Each of them is a facet of the love of God dwelling within, and each shines with a special beauty.

e. Commitment

It is important to make a commitment to develop a serious prayer life. Charismatics can take no more important step to love God or neighbor. It is valuable to be explicit because an explicit declaration of intention forces us to choose priorities and strengthens the will.

2. A Daily Pattern of Prayer

a. Morning Prayer

At its very outset, it is valuable to consecrate the day to Christ. The habit of beginning the day with prayer is important too. Morning prayer is best said upon rising and need only take a few minutes. It puts the day in proper perspective. Sometimes a note on a mirror or some other reminder will serve to stimulate the memory and assist in forming this very important habit.

A morning prayer should have these elements:
- Adoration of God.
- Thanksgiving for the night which has just passed and sorrow for any disloyalties or sins.
- Consecration of the coming day to Christ.
- A brief review of its events with special petitions for strength or whatever is called for, and mental notes about serious problems or potential obstacles to avoid.

b. Evening Prayer

A prayer period at the end of the day enables a person to sum it up and turn it over to God. It enables him to mend any errors or remedy any disloyalties which the day may have brought.

Evening prayers should include:
- Adoration and thanksgiving.
- A review of the day, calling upon God to bless those people we have met during the day and seeking forgiveness for failures or

disloyalties. This is the time to make earnest resolutions to do good and avoid evil.

● Commendation of oneself and all works and hopes to Christ.

● Consecration of the night to God and a request for his presence and protection.

c. Meditation

Here the name "meditation" is given to the central period of prayer in the day, although it involves more than meditation. This period is the heart of a vital prayer life. To be effective, it should last at least 20 consecutive minutes. It also helps to pray at the same time each day, preferably toward the beginning before the major tasks begin. It should take place in a location conducive to prayer.

This period is essential for Christian growth. It is usually necessary to begin by recognizing the need for such a time period, committing oneself to it, and seriously setting about to find a time and place in which it can really happen. Today lives are so tightly scheduled that most people balk at the idea of a regular time of prayer. Nothing is more important. It is the cornerstone of a life of devotion; it is the heartbeat of the Christian life. Until a person prays regularly in this manner, he will not be fully open to God's grace. Most of us find a way to do what we want, even if it means a sacrifice such as getting up early or using a lunch hour or break period. This kind of resolve will lead to daily prayer. Husbands and wives can be of special help and encouragement in this practice.

A format for this prayer time is offered here, although only as a suggestion. Whatever aids in growing in love should be used, and whatever does not should be ignored. This period of prayer should begin by turning to God in the most complete manner possible. It is necessary to quiet oneself and to attempt to concentrate upon him. Whatever aids in recalling whose presence is sought and in strengthening one's purpose to go before him should be utilized. It may help to imagine him as a mighty king or a gentle shepherd and as such enter into his presence. If helpful, a song might be sung or a psalm or text from Scripture may be recited. Prayer in tongues may be of assistance in this as well.

Having turned to him, it is then possible to enter into the body of the period of meditation. For those unfamiliar with meditation, any good manual on prayer should be of help. St. Francis de Sales' *Introduction to the Devout Life* is especially recommended. Meditation will be of great value at this point. Because its purpose is to lift the heart into praise of God and into resolutions of love, it may at times be unnecessary. The purpose of all prayer and especially of meditation is to lead to an act of devotion to God. To do so, structure often is helpful. There are times, however, when God simply ignores structures and lifts one into his presence. At such times a format should not be clung to, but freely abandoned in the face of his abundant gift. Those times when it is possible to peacefully rest in God's presence should be welcomed as well, and the temptation to keep the time "occupied" with the stuff of piety should be firmly resisted. These are times, as it were, to simply enjoy the Lord's company in the stillness of our heart just as Mary did at Jesus' feet. This is indeed the better portion (cf. Lk. 10:42).

It is usually advisable to formulate some resolutions during prayer which bear on love of God in daily life. These resolutions should be clear, immediate, and practical. At the end of the day it should be possible to judge whether they have been fulfilled. It is hardly satisfactory to resolve: "I must love more." Much more practical would be a resolution to perform such-and-such an act of love in a specific relationship today. It is then possible to determine whether this resolution has been fulfilled at the end of the day.

A period of meditation should be ended in an appropriate manner not just by stopping abruptly. It may help to thank God, to implore his assistance and that of all the saints, and to make an act of consecration to him again. The Our Father and Hail Mary are good prayers with which to end this period of prayer.

Most charismatics find prayer meetings conducive to prayer. Some of the features and lessons which make prayer meetings helpful can be applied to daily personal prayer. Both are periods of prayer with a loose structure and considerable informality. During them, a person seeks to hear God's Word and take it to heart. The prayer meeting contains times of praise, silence, readings from Scripture, and sharings. Each of these means can also be effectively used in personal prayer. They should be employed as they are at a prayer meeting to foster a sense of worship and to facilitate the understanding of God's Word.

There is a need for flexibility in personal prayer. There will be times when it will help to have some regular format which can be used or when it may help to read. There will be other times when no device is necessary and our spirit will seem to soar like an eagle. Both over-structuring and under-structuring should be avoided. It is important to understand the reason for this time of prayer so as to be able to judge what is and is not appropriate at a given time. The goal of this prayer is simple and quiet union with God in which the mind and senses are quieted. In a sense, its end is to simply enjoy God's presence. Whatever draws one to spontaneous movements of love toward God is prayer, be it reading, a regular devotional practice, song, or meditating on his goodness and mercy. At times each will have a place. In this regard, prayerful reading of the psalms can be of great help. Slow and soft reading aloud is a time-honored way of prayer which also may be of help.

Distractions should not be a source of dismay. At the beginning of a serious life of prayer, especially after the charismatic experience, distractions may not be encountered. Sooner or later they will appear, but they are no reason for concern. In the face of distractions it is important simply to try to concentrate. God understands man's weaknesses. What matters most to him is the intention of the heart and perseverance. Oftentimes, distractions are best defeated by being overlooked or ignored. When one becomes aware of being distracted, it often helps to set it aside and return to prayer. It may seem at times that the period of prayer is the time when all of the day's plans and important events urgently present themselves for consideration. These matters may need serious reflection, but not at this time. They should be resolutely set aside. The problem of distractions emphasizes the importance of finding an appropriate place to pray. It is hard enough to combat internal distractions without having to worry about external ones which could be avoided. Here, too, the time of prayer is important. God deserves prime time, as it were, when a person is fresh and alert—

not time when he is weary and unable to muster even a normal amount of concentration.

Periods of dryness or emptiness should not be a cause of distress. With the first experience of the Holy Spirit, it often seems as if the secret of life has been captured and one has been initiated into the mysteries of prayer. Alas, all too soon it becomes clear that it is God's grace which sustains and lifts one up. There will be times when this grace is withdrawn. At such times, God will seem very far away. At these times there are often severe temptations to discouragement and distress. To yield to them, however, would be a mistake. These are times when God leaves one to struggle, so it appears, alone and without his help. In reality, he is very close, perhaps closer than at times when a person is confident of his presence. These times of dryness are given in order to purify the heart. God wants to cleanse motives so as to cause men to pursue him rather than the consolations to be found in prayer. He also permits these periods to strengthen resolve. At such times there seems to be no inner strength, and even the slightest movement of the heart requires great effort. This appearance is deceptive, however. In fact at such times great strength is revealed in turning to God despite the heaviness and in firmly resisting temptations of discouragement or despair. Perseverance at such times is especially pleasing to God. Furthermore there will be times of great interior desolation which are due to external events or else to some interior problem. At these times strength and consolation can be found in union with Jesus crucified. It is possible to unite oneself with Jesus on the cross and find solace by contemplating the depth of his love and mercy. A true devotion to the cross is a wholesome and healthy complement to the spiritual life and should be cultivated.

d. Acts of Worship and Love

By faithfully observing morning prayer, meditation, and evening prayer, the day for God has a basic skeleton. That skeleton needs to be filled in by movements of the heart throughout the day. In monastic communities over the ages there arose the habit of dividing the day into hours, at which time the whole community would cease work and turn to God. By this practice, the superstructure of morning and evening prayer, as well as devotion, was reinforced by other set times of prayer. Such practices were also adopted in secular life, and in villages and cities the church bells would toll the times of prayer. Although modern life is often too complex for such practices, the principle behind them should be seriously considered. It is important to determine how to apply it to daily life. The principle is the recognition of a need to fill the day with explicit prayers. There are times in every person's day when prayer is possible. Whatever one's life style or schedule, it is possible to train oneself to make a brief prayer at points throughout the day. If a routine is followed, it will not be difficult to set aside regular times for prayer. If one's schedule is less regular, it is possible to pause before undertaking major projects. Such moments of prayer do not need to be long if they are taken seriously. One must cease working and turn spirit and heart to God. Some formal prayer may prove helpful at such times, such as the Angelus, the Our Father, Hail Mary and Glory Be, or a psalm. At these times, whatever form is used, it is important to renew one's consecration to God and to make an act of love toward him.

In addition to these regular acts of prayer, there will be moments throughout the day when God draws our thoughts or attention to himself. It is important to be very loyal to such inspirations. They need not long detract one from the task at hand and often will fill one with a freshness and zeal which will enable him to complete it with great interior peace. Some object of devotion will often serve as a reminder which the Lord can use for this purpose. For example, some object, such as a cross, a picture of Christ, or a Bible might be placed in view in an unoffensive manner. To make such an object a matter of controversy, however, would defeat its purpose. This practice can serve as a vehicle to quiet one's spirit and as a source of peace amid labor. Christian song can also aid devotion. Even at busy times a song can offer comfort and recollection in Christ. Another good habit worth cultivating is the use of unexpected free times which occur throughout the day as occasions for devotion. For example, the times when we wait for someone or experience a delay can be put to work for God instead of dissipating them or turning back to a task. We can turn to God at such moments. These sweet interludes will be deep sources of grace and open inner stores of strength.

3. Specific Advice about Prayer

a. Aids in Devotion

After a time prayer may become more difficult than in the time immediately following the charismatic experience. A certain amount of structured prayer may then enrich prayer times which had been spontaneous. There will be times when prayer is impossible without the aid of structure. In such cases, some of the styles of prayer encouraged by the Church and practiced by Christians over the centuries can be profitably used. Some of these devotions will be mentioned here. The most prominent, of course, is the rosary. This prayer, which is basically a repetition of the scriptural prayers, the Our Father, the greeting of the angel Gabriel, and a doxology, has a wonderful effect on the spirit and deepens devotion. It is physical as well as spiritual and can be of aid in disposing oneself to God.

Devotion to Mary is a source of much confusion to Protestants and some Catholics today. It must sadly be admitted that some of the misgivings which Protestants have expressed have a basis in certain excesses of Marian devotion. But it also must staunchly be maintained that authentic devotion to Mary has been a special gift of Christ to his Church and especially to those close to him (cf. Jn. 19:25-27). Far from distorting the place of Christ as unique Savior and mediator of grace, devotion to Mary forms one in the deepest love and adoration of Christ. Mary, the human who was so close to him and whose life was one of total obedience to the Father, is an apt teacher if ever there was one. If there is benefit from association with holy persons—and there is—how can there fail to be benefit from association with Christ's Mother? If one is attracted to the rosary, this impulse should be followed. Although some find the recitation of the mysteries to be helpful, others find them distracting. One of the great benefits of the rosary is that it can quiet the senses and occupy the intellect in a minimal way so that one is able to turn interiorly to God in a fuller and freer act of love. The prayers should be said reverently, not in a rush, even if that means not completing the whole rosary.

Another devotion of value is the Stations of the Cross. By following Christ in his passion, step by step, a person is enabled to enter into it with him and so to share in his redemptive act. Prayerful attention to this devotion on Fridays has the meritorious effect of recalling weekly in a moving way the depth of God's love.

Other forms of prayer and devotion have much to offer, too. Written prayers and litanies, for example, have a role to play in the life of prayer, and it would be foolish to close oneself to them on the assumption that they are outmoded and made obsolete by the charismatic experience.

b. Regular Patterns

There is great value in a regular pattern of prayer. We need a certain schedule and order. This is evident in public and private life in the division of time into hours, days, weeks, months and seasons. Life functions in cycles, and so also must a prayer life. It is helpful to give special attention to certain aspects of God's work on certain days. For example, the practice of keeping Sunday as the Lord's day—a day of rest and prayer—is very important. Friday provides a commemoration of the Lord's death. Saturday is often dedicated to our Lady. These habits give a week a certain routine which can greatly aid the life of prayer. The practice of setting aside a more lengthy period of time for prayer once a week is also very valuable. For example, an hour of adoration in front of the Blessed Sacrament is a venerable practice. On a monthly basis, regular patterns can reinforce our devotions as well. Some special time set aside once a month for prayer and reflection, for example, can be important. Throughout the year, the Church calendar provides the great seasons of Advent, Christmas, Lent, Easter and Pentecost in order to focus attention upon special aspects of God's work. These seasons should affect our spiritual life. Furthermore, at important stages in life, a period of retreat and prayer is extremely valuable. Such regular patterns insure that the daily, weekly, monthly, and yearly cycles as well as major periods in life are surrounded by prayer. By building in times for reflection and evaluation, one's life can be more explicitly ordered to God's will. By focusing on a weekly and yearly basis on the great events of salvation, it is possible to participate more intimately in the mystery of Christ's redemption. No businessman would seriously run an enterprise without taking time to reflect on basic objectives and their achievement. Neither can a Christian seriously expect to grow in Christian character without taking time to reflect on where he is heading and how he is to get there.

c. Tongues and Prayer

The charismatic gift of tongues can be a useful part of one's prayer life. If a person has this gift, it may be wise to incorporate it into a regular regime of prayer, especially at times of worship and praise. Throughout the day as well, prayer in tongues can aid recollection and concentration on Christ. A person should not wait to exercise this gift until he "feels" like it. One of its primary purposes is as a gift of personal prayer, and anyone whom it aids in devotion should use it faithfully.

d. The Imagination

The imagination is important to prayer. It can be a source of distraction and a source of temptations. There will be times when it presents vivid distracting images. It can, however, also be used to draw one closer to God. By using it to imagine things which are conducive to living for Christ, the desire to serve him can be deepened. For example, to relive scenes in Scripture in the imagination may replace temptations with images which enkindle devotion. Some spiritual writers recommend imagining a place such as the foot of the cross, Gethsemane, or Cana to which a person can "retreat" mentally during the course of the day as a place of refuge and means of deeper union with Jesus.

e. Petition

One of the most common forms of prayer with which charismatics are familiar is the prayer of petition. It springs from the natural inclination of Christians to bring their needs to their Father.

By taking needs simply and directly to God, a person develops a childlike quality which can be very pleasing to him. Christians must learn to place everything in his hands and to look to him for "daily bread." However, the misuse of this prayer must also be avoided. It can be abused by neglecting normal and prudent courses of action in favor of a "blind trust" in God. God has provided men with many gifts and abilities of the natural order. Although not supernatural or extraordinary, these abilities and facilities are his gifts too, and they should be used. Excessive recourse to petition can also stunt the life of prayer. Although bringing needs before him in detail has merit, there is also merit in trusting that he is aware of our needs and those of others. These needs and specific intentions should not receive undue attention. The Mass provides a means by which to estimate the place of petitions. Petitions have an important role in the liturgy, but they are not as important as prayers of praise and thanksgiving. A similar balance should be struck in personal prayer.

f. Review of Conscience

In discussing evening prayer, a review of the day was recommended. There is a specific form which such a review can take that can be of special value in combatting sins or vices. This method is suggested by St. Ignatius and recommended in his *Spiritual Exercises*. It consists in focusing attention on a specific area and to seek God's grace and healing. In growing in the Christian life, there will be times when it will be necessary to address specific problems such as combating temptation. This method of review can be of great help and should be consulted.

g. Penitential Seasons

The seasons of penance which the Church recommends—Advent and especially Lent—are times which should be taken very seriously. They are times for weeding. No amount of weeding, of course, will insure the growth of fruit in our spiritual garden. As St. Paul says, a person can give all away and even surrender his body to be burned and still lack love (cf. 1 Cor. 13:3). But weeds can, if unchecked, hinder the growth of plants. From time to time in the spiritual life the weeds—faults and areas of difficulty—need to be pulled or else they will choke out the life of grace. Each Christian has various weaknesses which God allows to remain. It is necessary to struggle against them. At times they crop up, or our vigilance slips. These seasons offer a chance for a little prudent self-denial and mortification which will strengthen the resolve to resist weakness.

h. Getting Started

Getting started is more important than understanding everything about prayer. Prayer is not something to be understood well without praying. There is, of course, a certain body of conceptual knowledge about prayer which can be acquired. It can be of some help. Proficiency at prayer, though, is acquired through practice and God's grace. In prayer, as in most matters, one does not begin as an expert.

The best way to start is simply to begin. The charismatic experience often assists prayer and makes it less awkward, but there will always be a certain amount of awkwardness in beginning an activity which is unfamiliar. A person must make up his mind to start, commit himself, set a time, and begin. It will probably be several weeks before the strangeness wears off and more time before it becomes a habit. Instant results should not be expected, but deep changes will become apparent over a period of time as a person remains faithful to regular prayer. Patience is very important here. Often a person is willing—so he thinks—to do great things for God. What God wants, though, is fidelity in this little matter. There will be time, later, for the great things of the Kingdom. Prayer comes first.

These elementary reflections on prayer are intended to establish a conceptual foundation on which an effective prayer life can be built. It takes a number of years to build a real prayer life, and a person should not be discouraged at failures or disappointments. On the other hand, there are real graces available in the charismatic experience which can be of considerable importance in making a good start. It would be unfortunate if a charismatic failed to take advantage of them and neglected to channel the energies of his experience toward establishing a solid foundation in prayer. Prayer is a way of life and an attitude of spirit, and it must be cultivated seriously. Properly understanding its goal, the role of the intellect, methods and types of prayer is important. It also is important to commit the will to building a life of prayer. Prayer in this sense depends not so much upon one period of prayer a day but on forging a daily pattern of prayer in which many events throughout the day reinforce a commitment to prayer and recall the spirit to God in acts of love. Within this framework, regular times of meditation and morning and evening prayer are far more valuable. Growth in prayer requires common sense, good spiritual advice, and perseverance. Specific advice can be of great help at various points in prayer. It should be sought and used when helpful. No one, however, can build a life of prayer for another person. Its basis must lie in the depth of an individual's love of God and a desire to participate in the knowledge of him. From this love, a rich life of prayer will grow. Perseverance in the life of prayer will perfect this love.

B: Scripture

The essence of Christian belief is that God has revealed himself to men in a complete manner in the person of Jesus Christ. Like Judaism, Christianity is a religion of revelation. God has revealed himself to men through words and deeds. He called Abraham and through him formed a people consecrated to himself. Throughout the following centuries, God showed himself to Israel. He spoke through deeds of salvation and through the law and the prophets. Finally, he spoke to men through Jesus Christ who by word and deed brought to men the saving knowledge of God.

Scripture is the Church's privileged record of these words and deeds. It records God's saving acts and his words to Israel in the Old Testament. This body of Scripture was recognized by the Church from the time of Christ as a special heritage. Jesus knew the Scriptures, quoted them often, and prayed them. The early Christians nourished themselves on the Old Testament which, for them, was the whole of Scripture. The writings of the early Church are filled with quotations from the Old Testament. In a sense, the Christians understood the Old Testament to have been fulfilled in Christ. The New Testament contains the apostolic Church's recollections of Christ's words and deeds as well as intimate glimpses into its own life. This record, consisting of the Gospels, Acts, Epistles and the Book of Revelation, was written during the years following Christ's death. It did not represent a uniform project, as any cursory glance at the books and letters comprising it will indicate. These documents were written for various reasons and treasured and circulated until, with the passage of time, an accepted canon of Scripture was recognized by the Church as embodying the inspired teaching of the Holy Spirit.

Throughout the centuries, the Church has revered and honored Scripture as a privileged source of revelation. In every age, it is a vehicle which Christ, the Word of God, has used to speak his living Word to men. Scripture is a treasury of devotion, a source of revelation for the unbeliever, of strength for the wavering, of instruction for all. It contains a privileged message which commands the faith and reverence of all Christians. Scripture is not just a chronicle of events but an object of faith. God inspired it and has given it to the Church as a gift and channel of his living Word. The Word of God in Scripture must then be approached in an attitude of faith, allowing God to reveal himself through it. It must be taken as a source, forever firm and concrete, by which the Word of God can be approached. As such, it cannot be altered or explained away. In reading and understanding it serious effort is required to seek to be loyal in every way to the deposit of faith which it contains.

One of the most salutary effects of the charismatic experience of the Holy Spirit is the awakening of a deep love for Sacred Scripture. Scripture speaks powerfully to an individual as a result of this experience. It is common for charismatics to carry copies of Scripture with them and to refer to it often. Such a result is a wonderful indication of the authenticity of this movement.

Because of the fundamentalist origins of Pentecostalism, however, it is possible for certain spurious doctrines or interpretations of Scripture to attach themselves to this awakening devotion to Scripture. Therefore, it is necessary to attempt to suggest a context in which Scripture can be understood and can become a means of genuine devotion. It must be recognized, sadly, that many Catholics are deficient in their understanding of the Scriptures, and the practice of the Church has not always given adequate emphasis to personal reading of Scripture. Regrettably, Scripture has even been an issue of division and suspicion between Catholics and Protestants. On the Catholic side, there has been on the part of some a suspicion of excessive familiarity with the Scriptures. Even the most severe reactions to the dangers seen in the Reformation were clearly not prompted by an opposition to the reading of Scripture in principle.[1] Fortunately, the recent popes and the Council have rejected such false notions and have emphasized the important role of Scripture in the life of the Christian and seriously encouraged Catholics to read it. Pope Pius XII in his teaching urged: "It is the serious duty of the faithful . . . to make free and holy use of this treasure."[2] He encouraged Christian families to read Scripture "daily with piety and devotion."[3] The teaching and devotional life of the Church have been founded in the Scriptures; for example, the Divine Office is scriptural, and the Mass, the center of Catholic life, is deeply scriptural.

Having established the importance of Scripture in a life of genuine devotion, we will now attempt to make several points which will serve to add a perspective to its role in the Christian life and to offer advice on its use.

1. In Christ the revelation of God is brought to completion. He commissioned the apostles to preach the Gospel. In the power of the Spirit they proclaimed the Gospel which they received from Christ. They fulfilled their commission through oral preaching, teaching, and establishing patterns of life and worship in the assemblies and through those apostolic writers who were inspired by the Spirit to commit this message to writing. At the close of their ministry, the apostles chose successors who were entrusted with the task of preserving and teaching the full message of Christ (cf. 2 Tm. 2:2). Through the guidance of the Holy Spirit, the revelation which has come through the apostles has developed as the Church and its members have grown in their understanding of the message

of Christ and its implications. In the life of the Church tradition is the channel of revelation preserved by the Spirit. By the Spirit's action through this channel, for example, we know the books of Scripture and understand the nature of their inspiration more profoundly. That is not to say, of course, that every tradition is a source of revelation. Many traditions, however worthy, are only of human origin. It is not by Scripture alone that certainty regarding revelation is to be attained. Tradition and Scripture complement each other. Both are sources of revelation, and both should, as Vatican II reminds us, "be accepted and venerated with the same sense of devotion and reverence."[4]

2. Scripture requires interpretation. There is a commonly cited position by which individuals claim to live literally according to Scripture and reject any "man-made" interpretations of it. Such a position has its origins in disputes and disagreements over various issues and has marked a number of churches and sects. It often represents an attempt to adhere in a vital and living way to the Word of God in Scripture in the face of some liberal scholars and churchmen which has made a wholehearted faith difficult for many. As such, it is commendable. Often, however, the popular manner in which this position is formulated is nonsensical.

Scripture does not speak for itself. It is not a systematic teaching about how to live the Christian life or how to understand its implications. On some matters it says little, and on others it appears, at first, to be contradictory. Anyone, whatever he may say or think, who tries to live a Christianity informed by Scripture, by that very act interprets Scripture, translating its precepts and guidance into a course of action. An example may illustrate this point. One of the most important issues facing the early Christians was their relation to Judaism. As the question arose, the Church had to consider Christ's teaching. He had not marked out a clear course of action. The Gospels do reveal several principles at work in Christ's words and actions. Roughly speaking, these might be summarized as a respect and reverence for the Law and a freedom in interpreting its meaning and sorting out its essence from non-essentials. The Church had to puzzle over this issue for some time. Aided by the Holy Spirit, it decided upon an interpretation of Christ's teaching and formulated a course of action. This process was one of interpretation. A similar process must be adopted in understanding what the Scriptures have to say about any facet of the Christian life.

Interpretation does not mean, however, interjecting one's own ideas about the way things should be. Scripture must be approached in a spirit of faith which seeks to understand the teaching of Christ with real loyalty. Such an attitude is the only acceptable way in which a Christian can approach the Word of God in Scripture.

3. Interpretation is not a private affair. Individuals, of course, must apply Scripture as well as the whole teaching of Christ and the Church to their lives, but there is an authority which the Church has in interpreting Scripture. In forming his own opinion, a believer has an obligation to seek enlightenment from the understanding and teaching of the Church. For Catholics, who believe that the Holy Spirit works in the ministry of the shepherds of the Church, this teaching authority must be received with faith and obedience. This, too, is a way in which God speaks (Acts 20:28; 2 Thes. 2:15; 2 Pt. 1:20).

These points are proposed as a balance to the notion that Scripture is the sole authority for living the Christian life. It must be noted, however, that Scripture is an important authority for a Christian and that Christians must draw close to it if they would hear the Word of God. It should be read prayerfully so as to form and guide the heart.

4. It is little help to be exhorted to read Scripture without being told *how*. Several simple principles can be of considerable assistance in seeking to understand a particular text or passage from Scripture.

(a) It is necessary to read Scripture with eyes of faith. If there is any theme which unifies the Old and New Testaments, it is a call for a decision about God and his works. The New Testament especially is a call for commitment; it testifies to the saving works of God through Christ and invites a response of faith in him. As Dom Charlier has said: "The mentality of the Bible is one of challenge, one which demands commitment."[5] It is necessary to be receptive to this invitation if the message of Scripture is to be understood. It is, I believe, in ignoring this great truth that so many students of Scripture fall short. Cultivating a pseudo-scientific in-difference, they seek to divorce their approach to Scripture from their faith, which is a weak methodology for the scholar who would know Scripture and impossible for the Christian who must believe in it. These are words which give eternal life and should always be approached with great reverence and love.

(b) It is important for a person who is unfamiliar with Scrip-ture to be sure he understands what is being said or happening in a given passage. For example, in a text from Exodus or a passage from the Gospels, it helps to understand the external dynamics of the situation. Unfamiliar terms, names, or places may obscure this basic meaning. Most editions of Scripture have maps and glos-saries which should be used. Extremely complex passages should be avoided at first. As a simple rule, it will help to try to formulate in one sentence what is happening or what is being talked about.

(c) Ask yourself what the author was trying to say. The au-thors were writing to specific people with specific points in mind (cf. Lk. 1:1-4; 2 Cor. 2:1-4). It is not possible to understand the text without understanding their meaning. Interpretations based on how a passage strikes us without relating to the author's meaning are spurious. Pope Pius XII asserted: "The supreme rule of in-terpretation is to discover and define what the writer intended to express." He quotes St. Athanasius: "It should be noted on what occasion the apostle spoke: we should carefully and faithfully ob-serve to whom and why he wrote, lest being ignorant of these points, or confounding one with another, we miss the real meaning of the author."[6]

The text must also be considered in light of other related pas-sages in Scripture. Where there is some apparent contradiction, some attempt must be made to understand the difference and a reconciliation sought. Finally, the text should be considered in light of the interpretation given to it by the Church and other Christians over the centuries. Any good commentary will be of considerable assistance in this. Two popular Catholic commen-taries are *The Jerome Biblical Commentary* and the *Pamphlet Bible Series*. Peake's Commentary is a moderate, balanced com-mentary of Protestant inspiration which many Catholics also have found useful.

Patently, some texts are *not* meant to be taken literally. They represent a manner of speaking or making a point. Jesus does not expect Christians to mutilate parts of their bodies to avoid sins, although his words literally call for that (Mt. 5:29-30). He is making a point by hyperbole, exaggerating in order to demonstrate how seriously sin should be resisted. Similarly, in saying that no man should be called "father," Jesus does not mean that parents should no longer be called "father" by Christians (Mt. 23:9). St. Paul, in fact, uses this term in a spiritual sense to describe his relationship to the Corinthians (1 Cor. 4:15). Jesus speaks in this manner to emphasize the importance of the Fatherhood of God for Christians; he means that this relationship should be of the greatest importance. These examples are minor but they illustrate the potential difficulties to which a narrow interpretation of a given text can lead. In a more positive sense, though, a balanced interpretation of Scripture can enrich its meaning and significance for the Christian life. For example, acquaintance with Jewish practice and the liturgical practices of the early Christians can give the texts describing the Last Supper new power and vitality. Furthermore, acquaintance with the Old Testament, and especially with the Law, prophets, and psalms, offers considerable light on Jesus' teaching. Many editions offer cross-references to various texts in the New and Old Testaments. Careful examination of these references can be very fruitful. The footnotes of *The Jerusalem Bible* and *The New American Bible* are especially helpful and should be consulted especially for important texts.

5. Scholarship can make an important contribution to an authentic scriptural devotion. Strictly speaking, of course, scriptural scholarship is not at the service of Christian piety, and there have been occasions when it has raised unsettling questions which have disturbed faithful Christians. More often than not, however, these questions are the work of popularizers or pundits whose claim to serious scholarship is questionable. On the whole, the serious study of Scripture over the last one hundred years has tended to confirm and deepen the conviction of Christians as to the authenticity and depth of these unique holy books. For a believing Christian the fruits of genuine scholarship can lead to a deeper love of God and an increased ability to turn to him in obedience and faith.

6. An understanding of Scripture begins, of course, with familiarity with its basic make-up. A regular program of Scripture reading can also be helpful. A careful reading of the entire New Testament may be the best way to start. In doing so, the Gospels are the logical place to begin. These "books" are comparable to the length of a chapter in a modern book or novel. The entire New Testament does not take long to read. An adequate program of Scripture reading, though, should include the Old Testament as well.

The Church uses Scripture in many ways. The readings used in the daily and Sunday liturgies are a special means by which Scripture can be appreciated. In fact, following the texts used at daily Mass would be an excellent program of Scripture reading. These readings are available in a variety of places and represent a balanced approach to Scripture on a yearly cycle attuned to the liturgical seasons.

It is very important to own a good translation of the Bible. Four English Bibles are now in common use: *The New American Bible* by American Catholics, *The New English Bible* by English Protestants, *The Jerusalem Bible* by French and English Catholics, and the *Revised Standard Version* which is a modernization of the old King James. The reliability of the *Revised Standard Version* (RSV) has been established by several decades of scholarly use, whereas the other three are still in the process of evaluation. It is also important to begin a session of Scripture reading or study with a prayer. Pope Pius XII encouraged Christians to pray to the Holy Spirit in reading Scriptures. The reading of Scripture should, of course, be an integral part of the daily rhythm of prayer too. After a person is acquainted with the Scriptures in a first-hand manner, it will help to refer to secondary sources such as articles in commentaries and various studies.[7]

For a charismatic spirituality to be authentic, it must be nourished by Scripture. The Scriptures are not primarily a manual meant to equip a fervent evangelist, nor are they a source for apologetics and arguments to attack or support various points of view. They are a source of revelation about God and his Son, Jesus

Christ. Through an intimate familiarity with Scripture, a charismatic can be formed in mind and heart in the knowledge of Jesus. The charismatic experience provides great graces which can increase or form an intimate love of the Scriptures. These graces should be cultivated, and charismatics should go to the Scriptures daily for consolation, renewal, and strength. Although they can be abused or misused, the Scriptures are an important source of life which cannot be ignored without sad deficiencies by a serious Christian. In reflecting upon the importance of Scripture, Vatican II echoed the words of St. Jerome: "Ignorance of the Scriptures is ignorance of Christ" (Rv. 6:25). Put in a positive sense, Scripture is a door to the personal knowledge of Christ and his work in the world. For charismatics who wish to grow in the knowledge and love of Christ, Scripture offers a privileged means to growth.

C. The Sacraments

In living a life of devotion, a Christian should have frequent recourse to the sacraments. They are special channels of grace which Christ has given to men through the Church. All of the sacraments are vital to Christian piety in practical ways. The graces of these sacraments can be claimed with considerable profit, and it is important to form oneself in a sacramental spirituality. The graces of baptism and confirmation are sources of strength in living out the Christian life. By calling upon Christ and claiming their graces, it is possible to serve God with renewed vigor. The Church recognizes and encourages this practice in the annual renewal of baptismal vows at Easter. The graces of the sacrament of matrimony are of tremendous help in living out the married vocation. These graces, as well as those of holy orders for deacons and priests, assist in living a way of life. This assistance can be sought and received. These sacraments are meant to be sources of strength far beyond the day on which they are conferred.

The Eucharist, however, is available to Christians in a more immediate fashion than the other sacraments. Through it, Christ intends to nourish men on their journey through life. One of the fruits of the charismatic renewal has been a fervent devotion to the Eucharist. Regular reception of this sacrament is an important aid to devotion. Jesus is the bread of life, and through the Eucharist he nourishes those who come to him. This sacrament is a profound source of life and healing. Prayer in the presence of the Blessed Sacrament is also an important form of Catholic piety. This devotion is honorable, and such prayer can enrich the spiritual life. By so doing, it is possible to approach Jesus in a simple and direct manner.

Penance, too, is an important source of grace. Through this sacrament, Christ forgives sins and heals. Penance should be used regularly and with faith. Care should be taken, whenever possible, to find a confessor who will provide helpful spiritual advice. A person should entrust himself to such a confessor and not make confession a mechanical operation, but a true means of repentance, reform, and growth.

D. Prayer with Others

Public assemblies for prayer are an important part of Christian devotion. The public prayer of the Church, the liturgy, is a special source of grace for the Christian. Through it, individuals and assemblies join with the universal Church in a prayer of adoration and praise to God. The prayers of the Divine Office and especially Morningsong (Lauds) and Evensong (Vespers) are very valuable forms of liturgical prayer. The practice of praying these prayers should be fostered whenever possible. Some churches still preserve the admirable custom of reciting Sunday vespers. The principal prayer of the Church, though, is the Mass. In this prayer, the entire Church joins in an act of homage and praise. Worship at Mass is the central act in a life of devotion.

It is important to realize that the Mass is a prayer offered by the whole Church. The changes in the liturgy are intended to encourage participation in this prayer. To be effective, they require cooperation. We should prepare for Mass by recollecting ourselves, using the preparatory rites. The entrance song can draw us consciously into God's presence. With the priest and congregation we acknowledge our sinfulness in the penitential rites. The Word of God in Scripture should be attended to as well as the priests' homiletic reflections on it. We should attempt to understand God's message to us through his Word as it is proclaimed and explained. The various prayers of the eucharistic liturgy invite prayerful attention. A Christian should reverently follow the canon, recalling Christ's gift of himself, and respond interiorly and orally with generosity and love. The Eucharist should be received prayerfully, and its reception should be followed by a time of profound thanksgiving.

Much has been written concerning the renewal of the liturgical life of the Church. Some of it is helpful, and the changes which have occurred have recalled Catholics to the importance of the Mass as a corporate act. However, it is a corporate act of worship. In addition to being a close-knit group of people—a community—it is necessary to worship as a community. Inner responses to the external aspects of the liturgy can enable us to enter into a spirit of worship. These habits can be cultivated, though they take time and some effort. They are important to develop.

Charismatics, especially, should be able to promote worship. The charismatic renewal offers a wonderful insight into the dynamics of a worshiping assembly. These lessons can be applied to the celebration of Mass and by personal example and sharing insights with others where appropriate. Prayer meetings, though not part of the official public prayer of the Church, do have an important place in a charismatic spirituality. Their spontaneous nature offers a valuable insight into worship and effectively complements other more formal modes of worship. They will be treated in Chapter 6.

E. Spiritual Reading

A regular program of spiritual reading can be of great value in growing in holiness. Spiritual reading differs from study in that its goal is to lead to a fervent love of God. It is not possible to prescribe a list of books which will assist everyone, but it is possible to suggest some principles and to recommend some titles. (Cf. "Recommended Reading" at end of book.)

Spiritual reading should be part of the normal cycle of prayer. It is important to take time to read. Reading can form a part of daily prayer. At times it will deepen prayer, and at other times it prevents serious distraction. Retreats are opportunities to do spiritual reading; it helps to bring along a book, and it helps to have a book ready at home too. When an opportunity to read presents itself, many people spend too much time wondering what to read. It makes sense to read different types of books. Lives of the saints or stories which are inspirational are an important type of spiritual reading. Such works often make interesting reading too. Other works should be read in different ways. Some manuals or works of instruction should be read slowly and in sections. Their message and lessons should be applied to daily life. The teachings of the Church and the letters and addresses of the leaders of the Church can also be sources of spiritual refreshment. Catholics as well as other Christians will find in them sources of great inspiration and comfort. For example, the documents of Vatican II or the weekly sermons of Pope Paul VI are sources of spiritual support.

F. Study

Study is an important part of the spiritual life. Since there normally is so little time for it, though, it is wise to formulate an approach to the study of Christianity which will enable a person over a number of years to be exposed to every aspect of Christian doctrine and practice. In choosing areas of study, a solid grasp of basic doctrine is more important than familiarity with peripheral controversies. In choosing authors, those who are sensational or who popularize theology at the expense of content and truth are best avoided. The time framework for a course of study should be broad enough to enable a person to cover an area; it should be based on a realistic estimate of what can be covered in a year's time. The following areas deserve consideration: Scripture, theology, the liturgy, spirituality, and Church history. A person should aim at an intelligent grasp of the central issues and problems involved in each area. Fortunately, there is available some popular literature which can serve as a guide. One of the principal aids in the study of Christianity will be the documents of Vatican II. These documents represent a privileged Word of the Lord to the Church in modern times. Anyone who is interested in Christian renewal and study should acquaint himself with these documents, especially the *Constitution on the Church*.[8] They steer a course which is both deep and wise, avoiding the errors of those who would compromise essential truths and those who would identify truths too completely with cultural forms or outmoded practices.

G. Specific Advice to New Charismatics

a. Avoiding Excesses

A tactic which Satan often uses is to drive a person to extremes. For example, penance is good in moderation. Satan would rather that a person did not do penance. But if we are resolved, he will then encourage us to overdo it and thus hopefully cause harm. After receiving the charismatic experience of the Spirit, people sometimes are less aware of human limitation and make unrealistic demands upon themselves. It is important to exercise normal prudence, especially in regard to mortification.

b. Discernment about Poverty and Vocations

For many the charismatic experience of the Spirit is a time of great zeal. It is important to try to be as generous with oneself as possible, but it is also necessary to recognize that many of the options which seem good at that time may not be from God. There are for example, among Catholics, standard reactions to a religious experience which in themselves have great merit, but which need to be tested carefully. The two most serious are a desire for poverty and a desire for a religious vocation. There is an association in most Catholics' minds between Christianity and poverty. There is much merit in this association, and all are called to reflect in their lives the poverty of Christ, but such a reflection of poverty is not easily come by. It requires a deep sensitivity as to what God is calling for. To simply abandon responsibilities and to fail to take legitimate human needs into account can be a source of considerable difficulty and even scandal. Rash actions regarding the material order must be avoided, especially where there is responsibility for a family.

Single Catholic men and women often associate a religious experience with a vocation to the religious life, and it well may be

one. However, such a call needs to be weighed and tested. Whatever specific vocation God is calling us to, he is calling all to a
total devotion to consecrate oneself to his will, whatever that may
be. Sometimes in the midst of an experience we lose this perspective and are too concerned with narrowing the specifics. Sudden
decisions, for example about entering religious life or getting married should be avoided. These inspirations must be tested over a
period of time. These reflections are not, it must be noted, meant
in any way to slight a genuine vocation. They are offered in the
belief that such vocations are rugged calls and will become clear to
one who is seriously seeking God's will without that person taking
imprudent actions.

c. Seeking Mature Advisers

In the time after receiving the charismatic experience of the
Holy Spirit, it is advisable to consult with mature Christians who
can offer advice. This advice should be taken seriously. A person
can sometimes be the worst judge of matters pertaining to himself,
and under the elation of the charismatic experience he is liable to
misjudge some things. Regular consultation with a person who has
been living an interior life for many years will be of great benefit.
Before taking any major steps such counsel especially should be
sought. In seeking counsel, it is important to present relevant facts
as explicitly as possible. God does speak through the agency of
others in such situations. Often the advice of others reveals how
deeply we are attached to a certain course of action, but other
courses may open us more fully to God's will. If our advisor is not
a priest, it may be helpful to seek out a prudent priest in whom we
have confidence to take advantage of the sacrament of penance.

There is a distinction between spiritual advice regarding our
relationship with God and counsel of a more general sort affecting
practical decisions. Often general counsel can be of great benefit
with regard to daily living, relationships, career, and practical matters. In the communities which are forming in the wake of the
charismatic renewal, such advice is frequently available, as is considerable assistance from others in coping with varieties of problems. The prerequisites for someone giving such advice are a good

mind, balance, and maturity. In the beginning stages of the spiritual life, it is also possible to benefit from the advice and counsel of relatively mature Christians. But as one grows, wise spiritual persons should be sought out who can provide the delicate advice needed to grow deeply. Throughout the Christian life, the company of those who will help by advice and example to deepen the love of God should be sought and treasured.

Conclusion

A charismatic spirituality must be based upon a rich interior life. The various means of spiritual growth mentioned here can serve to cultivate true devotion. They are the ways in which the heart can reach toward its divine spouse. Jesus teaches: "Abide in me, and I in you. As the branch cannot bear fruit by itself, unless it abides in the vine, neither can you, unless you abide in me. I am the vine, you are the branches. He who abides in me, and I in him, he it is that bears much fruit, for apart from me you can do nothing" (Jn. 15:4-5).

Charismatics must have as their goal an abiding relationship with Christ. Jesus calls for a righteousness which exceeds that of the scribes and Pharisees (Mt. 5:20). He does not call for an increase in the quantity of devotion but in its quality. What Christ expects from charismatics is eager hearts ready to hear his Word. He wants men whose ears are trained, as it were, to identify his voice and who will receive him when he comes. The scribes and the Pharisees, for all they knew and did, did not recognize him when he came. They failed in what mattered most. Their love was not quickened by Jesus' presence. By seeking every means of lovingly abiding in his presence, drawing close to him, studying his Word, speaking to him and being taught by him in a daily and living way, we can avoid this disastrous failure. Of charismatics who are so loud—and rightly so—in their praises and so fervent in their piety, Christ will expect no less. Only the heart which is trained in devotion, however, will be quick to recognize the Beloved. Charismatics as well as all Christians would do well to take note.

IV
Guidance

A. God Wants To Lead Christians

The charismatic experience often arouses or deepens a realization of the direct and personal operation of the Spirit. It awakens an inner faculty by which the presence of the Spirit can be sensed in a new mode. Charismatics must learn to use this new sense by seeking to discern the meaning of the leadings and promptings. Of course, seeking God's will is the concern of every Christian, and the problem raised here is not new. It is, however, new to many charismatics who did not expect guidance in an intimate way for their personal lives, relegating such things to the saints. Indeed, there is a lack of much popular teaching about the experiential aspects of the Spirit's leading. There is even a tendency to reject the very idea of promptings or leadings as a false illuminism. Such a spirituality is unsatisfactory and not at all in accord with the experience and best spiritual teaching of the Church. As a result, the charismatic experience often forces a re-examinaton of encrusted positions and a return to deep and authentic teaching. Moreover, the charismatic renewal as an authentic outpouring of the Spirit poses new pastoral problems which call for a new formulation of this teaching in light of the experience of charismatics. We will not attempt a systematic treatise here but will rather formulate some principles which point toward an approach in this area that hopefully will be of value to those attempting to understand how to be loyal to the leadings of the Spirit.

The leadings of the Spirit must be understood in the broad context of God's saving purpose. From the beginning of the human race, the Scriptures testify to God's desire to guide his people. Despite men's sin and obstinacy, God steadfastly worked to show them how to live and intervened when they erred. In his love, he conceived a plan for man's salvation. His purpose was to restore the harmony that was broken between God and man and to enable man to be happy. It was his gracious intention not only to restore man to his pristine state, but to elevate him to a participation in his very life. He unfolded this plan by calling forth a people through Abraham and his descendants. Again and again he revealed himself to his people by raising up leaders for them and speaking to them through prophets. Throughout this time, it was he himself through the agency of these leaders who "led forth his people like sheep, and guided them in the wilderness like a flock" (Ps. 78:52). He was for them "Savior and Redeemer" (Is. 60:16). Not content, however, with working through intermediaries, he intended to lead them directly and in person. He foretold this through the prophets: "I myself will be the shepherd of my sheep, and I will make them lie down, says the Lord. I will seek the lost, and I will bring back the strayed, and I will strengthen the weak, and the fat and the strong I will watch over" (Ez. 34:15-16).

God manifested himself by taking flesh in the person of Jesus. He personally came to lead and save his people. He is the good shepherd (cf. Jn. 10:1-15). Through the saving work of Christ, God's salvation became available not just to the physical descendants of Abraham but to all the nations. Jesus promulgated a new law or covenant which fulfilled the law of Moses and completed the work of the prophets.

The scope of God's Saving Plan, then, was vast. He had personally revealed himself by becoming a man, and he extended to all men the offer of salvation and new life. The saving work was not confined to objective exterior actions. He sought to lead his people interiorly and intimately as well. His message through the law and the prophets was not simply or primarily concerned with exterior matters. It was a moral and spiritual revelation ordered to evoke a renewed and deepened relationship between himself and his people. Through Jesus' gift of the Holy Spirit, the intimate and personal nature of God's work was made apparent. His guidance was to be in the deepest and richest way. He had chosen to dwell with each believer and to make his home with him (Jn. 14:23). God, then, has intended that men should know him. He has revealed his will to them by the most radical means. Rather than a distant deity, he has proved himself to be a God who speaks and acts directly, personally, and intimately in the lives and affairs of men.

It is natural to expect that a God so eager to guide and save would work in the life of an individual in a direct and immediate way. In addition to the hidden, indirect ways he works through nature and providence, God manifests himself explicitly in the life of a believer, and these manifestations are not rare or unusual. All too often Christians content themselves with a notion of a God who is distant and who has little to do with the daily workings of their lives. Regrettably, we find a certain comfort in such a notion of God, the divine programmer who mysteriously pre-programs us and then steps out of the picture. This sterile interpretation of God's actions is not consistent with the active and powerful record of God's intervention in the affairs of men which the New Testament offers. The early Christians knew God and had daily intercourse with him. The incidents recorded almost casually in Acts and the Epistles show us how much God's intimate presence was taken for granted. A few passages will illustrate this point: Peter filled with the Spirit in speaking to the Sanhedrin (Acts 4:8); the disciples in prayer (Acts 4:31); the story of Ananias and Sapphira (Acts 5:1-11); Stephen's martyrdom (Acts 7:55); Philip's ministry to the Ethiopian eunuch (Acts 8:26-40); Peter's experience with Cornelius (Acts 10:1-11:19).

The authors of Scripture presumed on the part of their readers an acquaintance with the manifest workings of God. The early Christians were conscious of God's power in deed. They were also well aware of God's interior workings and spoke of them in forthright terms. The scriptural accounts reveal a consciousness of the presence and working of God fully consistent with his promises and his past behavior. Nothing has happened to suggest that he has changed his mode of operation. In fact, the experience of Christians throughout the ages reinforces this expectation that God manifests himself in explicit ways to his people. If the common experience of Christians today is different, we must face the fact that our situation is unusual. We must ask whether there may not be a deficiency in our ideas or expectations. To be sure, we have not ceased to believe theoretically that God speaks and acts and even that he speaks personally in a way that can be intelligently grasped. Do we ever put this theory into practice? It is one thing to admit that God can lead, and quite another to hold that he does and should as a normal part of a Christian's life. It is necessary to confess the poverty of a Christianity which removes us from a living consciousness of the presence of God and an expectation of his guidance. Furthermore, modern life does little to awaken us to an awareness of God's guiding presence and often stifles it. Jesus has made it clear, however, that God wants to guide and direct his people in an intimate and immediate way. It is important for Christians to open themselves to his guidance and to cultivate an awareness of it.

Guidance in this sense refers not so much to the dramatic or spectacular but to an active and regular experience of the reality and guiding presence of God. This guiding presence is most often plain and unexciting in appearance and rather unlike the histrionics our imaginations might lead us to expect. It is, however, consistent with the humble and gentle manner in which he has revealed himself in Christ. Even if the wrapping is simple, the contents are not necessarily plain. God's leadings may be in normal, regular, and ordinary ways as well as the more dramatic ones, but it is God nonetheless, and even the most ordinary of his acts is fraught with special implications. The emphasis in the charismatic renewal upon seeking divine guidance is a wonderful remedy for much that is blasé in modern Christianity. The charismatics' appreciation of God's ability to work through leadings and signs is also a relief in a world which has shut God out. Although the experience of charismatics requires balance, it is to be welcomed as a happy and timely consequence of the Spirit's work.

B. Following the Leadings of the Spirit

Having recognized that God wants to guide Christians in an intimate and personal way, it is necessary to consider how to identify and interpret his guidance. Following the Spirit is a process that requires hard work and faith. It calls for a sensitive discernment of his leadings and prayerful judgment of all of the many factors involved in knowing God's will. God guides men through the process with signs and gentle leadings. He does not generally give individuals absolute certainty but lets them grope step by step, fortified at times only by faith in him.

God's will, of course, is simple. He works in simple and direct ways while men are complex. His will, simple in itself, must be broken down into bits and pieces corresponding to the contingencies of time and space with which men are familiar. Furthermore, God takes into account hesitations and disloyalties. His goal is not to force something upon men but to lead them freely to choose his will. Our free cooperation is an integral part of this process. As a result, at times his will appears most opaque.

1. Special Considerations in Following the Spirit's Leadings from a Charismatic Perspective

Charismatics may object that their experience proves that the will of God can be readily known and that it is easy to follow the Spirit. Their experience does add another proof to the argument that the will of God and the leadings of the Spirit can be known. It does not prove that knowing or following them is an easy matter. In fact, their experience, admittedly limited, tends to establish the contrary.

In the wake of the charismatic experience, of course, matters can appear different to a new charismatic. The leadings of the Spirit are abundant and God's will seems easily understood and obeyed. We have spoken of a honeymoon period of grace operative immediately after the charismatic experience which provides a foretaste of the full Christian life. During this time, the leadings of the Spirit are often manifest and God's will can seem apparent. In time, however, the normal economy of grace reasserts itself and a person is left to decipher God's will as best he can. In addition, there is also a certain naiveté on the part of new charismatics. The excitement of the experience heightens the new charismatic's expectation of the unusual, and it is easy to see everything through glasses which give events a "super-spiritual" glow. For example, the hand of God becomes "obvious" in the most ordinary coincidence, or God speaks "clearly" through signs which are often am-

biguous. While it is disconcerting to some, such a tendency is understandable and even somewhat amusing. In a short time this
over-spiritualization usually passes. Somewhat embarrassed, a person begins to realize that some of the "leadings" so gleefully
grasped may have been empty, meaningless distractions, or even
sources of confusion and dissipation, while others are valid. It then
begins to dawn upon him that sensing leadings of the Spirit is only
part of the process of knowing God's will and that extraordinary
leadings are only one kind of leading. God's will then appears less
obvious, not black or white, but something to be seriously sought.

For new charismatics, the process of understanding God's will
is often one which requires considerable adjustment. The charismatic experience opens a new dimension. Our decision-making
process is often thrown into a new balance. When this is a major
transition, there will be temporary turmoil and confusion. Such
disruptions normally attend major personal adjustments. Nor is it
unusual during this time for there to be emotional highs and lows.
Times of great enthusiasm can be sharply succeeded by times of
discouragement. It is important at such times to recognize God's
desire to lead us and to seek to cultivate a deep desire to be led by
him. Cooperation with his leadings takes time. At the outset, it is
important to be patient and to avoid discouragement. Following
the Spirit is like learning to walk; it takes time, trial, and error.
Once mastered, though, most children find walking superior to
crawling; so will charismatics. It is important to persevere in seeking to know God's will and the leadings of the Spirit whatever set-
backs or frustrations are encountered. Knowledge of God's will is
the mark of Christian maturity (Heb. 5:14; 1 Cor. 2:12-16), and an
awareness of the Spirit's leadings is an important facet of knowing
God's will.

a. Two Tendencies

It might be valuable, at this point, to note two tendencies
which affect openness to the leadings of the Spirit.

Individuals with strong, dominant personalities are probably
less inclined to be open to the leadings of the Spirit. Used to making their own decisions and independent, they are not easily led.

On the other hand, weaker personalities who find decisions hard to cope with are at times all too happy to use the leadings of the Spirit as an escape from making hard choices. Different advice, of course, is required for these tendencies. The strong person needs to let God work and direct. He must learn patience, meekness, and humility. Even after becoming accustomed to seeking the leadings of the Spirit, he will tend to rush into projects, force issues, and seek results. These qualities are not at all bad, but they need to be curbed and disciplined. An individual with such strength needs to learn to wait on the Lord and will probably struggle many years to learn this lesson. Weaker personalities will also have a long struggle, although it will be in the opposite direction. They will learn that God wants them to grow in making decisions. He will want to strengthen their character. For them, his grace and leadings will be ordered toward acting. He will want them to choose a direction for themselves. These examples are abstract, and the two tendencies often co-exist in the same person. An individual may be strong in some areas and weak in others. It should be understood, though, that God wants to work in men in order to bring about a wholeness, moderating excesses and strengthening weaknesses of personality.

b. Super-Spiritualism: A Danger

Super-spiritualism is an equation of knowing God's will with sensing spiritual leadings. Charismatics are prone to such tendencies because of their familiarity with the Spirit's leadings and the emphasis given to striking manifestations. Encouraged by sloppy or incorrect teaching, they can develop a spirituality which emphasizes the leadings of the Spirit in an unhealthy way. Seeking God's will then becomes primarily a matter of sensing promptings and acting upon them. To follow the Spirit, they must abandon the use of reason. Any coincidence or accident becomes God's will. For example, a text received may mean more than what others, the whole teaching of Scripture, or common sense tells them. Or they could set out with one course of action in mind and end up doing the opposite. They are blindly governed by interior leadings and incapable of long-range consistent action. Such an approach is an affront to a serious Christian and makes a mockery of following the leadings of the Spirit. It is superstitious and can be an escape from responsibility. The person who does this is in his own magical kingdom, a kingdom which has little to do with the Kingdom of God. God's work appears like a magic puppet show in which God is behind the scenes, pulling the strings. This approach is sometimes difficult to identify at once because it can resemble an authentic and sane spirituality in some respects. Over a period of time, though, its consistency and shallowness become evident. It is dangerous because by relying solely on interior and spiritual leadings it runs the twofold risk of mistaking any inner leading for God's leading and of ignoring the external ways he has of revealing his will. It takes considerable maturity to distinguish between various impulses and spiritual leadings. Super-spirituality appears in various degrees in the charismatic movement and should be resisted firmly because of the harm it can cause to individuals and the discredit it can bring on a genuine spirituality.

2. Following the Leadings of the Spirit

The leadings of the Spirit are of great importance in seeking to know God's will. A leading of the Spirit is a particular revelation of God in Christ. Through a leading God guides individuals or groups in an immediate and personal manner toward his will embodied as a particular objective not readily apparent through, but consistent with, the channels of nature, reason, and the deposit of the faith. These leadings are a way that God manifests his love and seeks to lead his people. For an individual, they must be viewed in the context of seeking God's will. For the whole Christian people they are one way in which God manifests his shepherdship. They complement the normal channels through which he works and leads such as the sacraments, Scripture, and the bishops.

a. Ordinary and Extraordinary Leadings

The ordinary means by which the Spirit leads are familiar and have been discussed at length in previous chapters. They include a regular life of prayer, Scripture, the sacraments, spiritual direction, study, and community. God uses them as a means to lead men. A regular life of prayer is the most important of these vehicles. Through a life of prayer, we can come to know the Lord's voice and distinguish it in a personal way. For example, in receiving the Eucharist, we may be drawn to adore the presence of Christ. We may have an abstract faith in his presence, but the Spirit uses this opportunity to unfold this truth in a deeper way. A text encountered in the ordinary reading of Scripture may speak in a special way, causing a deeper personal surrender to God. Or a homily may be the occasion for a special insight and prompting for a charitable deed. The name "ordinary" is misleading if it implies something which any man can know unaided. On the contrary, these "ordinary" leadings depend upon the very special revelation of God in Jesus Christ and the work of his grace. They are privileged vehicles of grace which should not be slighted.

In addition to these ordinary means through which God leads, there are extraordinary or charismatic means as well. The extraordinary means are distinguished from the ordinary because they require a special work or movement of the Spirit. We do not have access to these means of discerning the leadings of the Spirit in the same way that they have access to the normal means which God uses. There are times when God leads powerfully through them and other times when he does not use them or when they do not seem to convey any clear direction. Since the extraordinary means have not been examined previously, we will consider them carefully.

An extraordinary leading of the Spirit is a means which the Spirit has of revealing God's will to us in a fashion more apparent than through the ordinary leadings. The extraordinary leadings are special movements of grace not always available to us. The Spirit can use things which otherwise might be ordinary channels of grace or the normal circumstances and occurrences of our lives. They are best understood in the relationship with the ordinary leadings, but it may help to seek to isolate them first. These leadings can be treated under three categories: (1) interior promptings of the Spirit; (2) exterior promptings (including hearing something from someone and providential signs); (3) actively seeking guidance.

1. *Interior Promptings of the Spirit.* The charismatic experience is accompanied by a great sensitivity to the interior promptings of the Spirit. An interior prompting is a means by which the Spirit seeks to lead a person through leadings apparent to the inner self. Interior words, audible words (heard only by the one addressed), impulses, dreams, visions, and anointings are examples of such promptings. These means are used frequently in Scripture and are well known by spiritual writers. Because they are illusive and intangible, they are somewhat unsettling to many people. The object of promptings may differ. Some are ordered toward some type of outward action, while others are directed toward inner movements of love. Although these means are grouped together, they are of differing quality, and all require testing. Generally, if their object is an interior disposition of love toward God or a person, we need be less cautious with them than if they call for some dramatic response. Where they work in some way to make known God's intentions, they should be tested in the same fashion as suggested later for the charismatic gifts; in fact, in such situations they may be gifts for a particular group. For example, visions have sometimes been shared at prayer meetings with great profit. They have much the same effect as prophecy. Where a leading calls for action, it must be tested with caution. Impulses are not necessarily from God. Dreams can be from God but need to be received as divine messages with great care. Over a period of time it usually becomes clear if they are reliable channels of the Spirit's leadings.

Anointings are commonly spoken of by charismatics. Sometimes the word is used generally to describe any leading or even the overall process of discernment by which a person makes a decision. There is, however, an interior anointing commonly experienced. An anointing is an interior prompting accompanied by some physical sensation. Its essence is not the physical sensation, however, but the presence and movement of the Spirit. Sometimes the sensation resembles being covered with oil, the source of the name. This leading can be understood as an experiential participation in Christ's anointing. Christ means "the anointed one." He has been anointed by the Father with the Holy Spirit, and as members of Christ's body we share in that anointing. The prompting of which we speak is an experiential awareness of this reality.

2. *Exterior Promptings.* Actually the term "exterior promptings" is incorrect. It is used for convenience. It indicates that things exterior to the individual are being used by the Spirit in such a manner as to create an inner awareness of the Lord's will.

An exterior prompting frequently experienced by charismatics is hearing something from someone. Of course, we hear things from others most of the time. This prompting occurs when the Spirit uses ordinary communication to speak to us with a force and immediacy out of proportion to the situation. In such a situation, it will be obvious to us that the speaker is being used as an agent. Testimonies, sharings, sermons, prophecies, or counseling can be occasions for such promptings. In fact, any form of communication can be used. The speaker himself is often unaware of how the Spirit is using his words. One instance of such a prompting would be a situation where a speaker addressing a general audience says something which strikes home as if he were speaking only to us and could see our inner thoughts. There is an efficacy here for the person addressed. The Spirit has used these words to speak to him in an extraordinary way.

God also uses other things which are exterior to speak to us in an extraordinary way. Providence, of course, pertains to the ordinary way in which God directs us and cares for us. In the course of this ordinary direction, there can be signs which he uses. There are, however, instances when he uses providential signs as a means of an extraordinary leading. In such a case, the sign serves as an occasion for the Spirit to speak to us in a more immediate and direct manner than would otherwise be warranted. For example, several unrelated coincidences could serve to confirm a given course of action. The statements made above regarding interior leadings can also be made about these leadings. They need to be tested and can point to different objects.

3. *Actively Seeking Guidance.* The two general means which we have considered above are initiated by God. What distinguishes the type of extraordinary leading we speak of here is that it is initiated by us. It is clear that we must not test or try God. Yet there are occasions when he permits us to look to him for assurance and

guidance in a more direct manner than usual. Although such activity might sound sacrilegeous or potentially superstitious, it can be pleasing to God if accompanied by the proper interior attitude.

The motive which must govern our actions in such an instance is a humble loving desire to know his will. We should go to him as a father like little children. We should be confident in his goodness and plan and have faith in him while recognizing that he may not choose to speak in such a way. While it cannot be said that we should be inspired to go to God in such a manner, an inspiration would be a factor in a decision to take such a step. There is a difference, too, in the manner in which we seek God's will. There is a considerable difference, for instance, between what is known as setting a fleece before the Lord and praying from a text in Scripture. The term "fleece" is taken from the story of Gideon who set out a fleece as a test to ascertain God's will. One night he asked that the dew fall on the ground and not the fleece. The next night he asked that the dew touch the fleece but not the ground. Each day he awoke to find that his prayer had been answered, and he took this as a sign from the Lord. It is not proper to set out a fleece arbitrarily in the face of every decision. However, it is difficult to set out in an abstract manner principles by which to determine when it is proper or improper in a given situation. The factors which lead us to do so in a given situation should be thoughtfully examined and reflected on later in light of what happens. It is also difficult to give an absolute answer as to what to conclude when the Lord does not respond to a fleece. We may have been mistaken in setting one out in the first place. Generally, it might be said that we are safer in this course of action if we have already prayerfully sought to discern God's will and fixed upon a course of action as a result of an inspiration to do so in order to ascertain the correctness of our discernment. It is usually advisable to consult with a prudent Christian before doing so. Seeking guidance from Scripture is much less arbitrary since it involves turning to God's Word. Nor does it involve specifying something as a sign. This practice can be greatly beneficial and has been used by several saints. It, too, is subject to abuse, however. Here general prudence and common sense must be used. These matters are treated more directly later.

Extraordinary and ordinary leadings can work together in marvelous harmony. For example, a prompting of the Spirit can point toward a course of action. Through prayer and consultation with a spiritual director and another mature Christian, a person may decide that this is the course which God wishes him to follow. By prayerful reflection he then may map out a series of steps. In the course of this planning, God may give him a specific insight which deepens or completes his action through some extraordinary leading. This example illustrates the way in which God can use both these means to reveal his will. In the normal Christian life, they complement each other. The term "extraordinary" or charismatic is not meant to imply infrequency or dramatic effects. In fact, extraordinary leadings can occur often. They simply cannot be counted on as regular or dependable channels. The ordinary means serve like a skeleton to give a fundamental shape and structure.

The use of these two types of leadings might be compared to following a complicated route. There may be a map to follow, but from time to time it helps to stop to check the route and to ask for directions. These two methods are used in a complementary manner to achieve an end. Both ordinary and extraordinary means are given to lead us to God. On the whole, the ordinary means should be given greater weight. Although not absolute, it is generally true that any charismatic leading will be supported through the ordinary means by which God leads. An impulse supported and reinforced by an ongoing prayer life, for example, is to be taken much more seriously than an unsupported impulse. We have already mentioned the consequences of excessive reliance on leadings. It must be pointed out that there is, however, a dangerous tendency among some charismatics to overemphasize the role of leadings of the Spirit and especially the extraordinary ones. They have become the object of a cult in which no action would be entered upon without seeking a leading. Seeking leadings excessively can cause confusion and turmoil. It is too often the case that errors in judgment are made by charismatics through an improper regard for the normal means which God has of leading. Charismatics must seek to cultivate a healthy respect for the ordinary workings of the Spirit and seek to develop a balanced approach to this entire area.

In addition, it must be cautioned that anyone with emotional problems should carefully avoid seeking leadings without mature and prudent counsel.

b. *Identifying the Leadings of the Spirit*

Identifying the leadings of the Spirit presents a major problem to most charismatics. It is an area in which hard and fast rules cannot be formulated. Nevertheless, some general advice can be given.

Leadings need to be tested. Just because an individual receives an impulse which he thinks is spiritual does not mean it should be acted upon. It is important to subject a leading to careful scrutiny because it is possible to be misled or to mislead oneself. A person can read a false significance, for instance, into events or situations which they do not themselves contain and be misled. In this case, the interpretation is from personal sources rather than divine ones. Impulses, too, can come from a variety of sources. Leadings can be a product of one's own interior make-up, flowing, for example, from emotions, intellect, or imagination. They can also come from others or ideas to which one may be exposed. Furthermore, leadings can come from spiritual sources other than God.

The notion of evil spirits has been derided as a hold-over from the pre-scientific past. The credentials which this notion possesses, however, are too impressive for it to be exorcised by a theory of human enlightenment. Christ and his Church take such spirits in deadly earnest. It would be foolish not to recognize that they can be the source of spiritual impulses. St. John warns Christians: "Do not believe every spirit" (Jn. 4:1), and St. Paul advises the Thessalonians to "test everything" (1 Thes. 5:21). An individual open to the leadings of the Holy Spirit can be tempted by evil spirits as well. Indeed, St. Paul warns that Christians contend not with flesh and blood but "against the powers, against the worldly rulers of this present darkness, against the spiritual hosts of wickedness in the heavenly places" (Eph. 6:12).

It is therefore important to subject any leading to scrutiny. In the first place, it is necessary to identify a leading. Some leadings are strong and self-evident and easily recognized. Others are less so. A timid or unconfident person may be less inclined to admit that a given impulse is a leading than a self-confident person. In order to identify a leading, there need only be a reasonable suspicion that it is authentic. If an individual asks for God's light, tries to be objective and still feels the presence of a leading, that leading should be taken seriously.

There is an interior test for leadings which is sound if not infallible. The love of God and Christ's peace are two marks of Christ's work. A leading is like a spontaneous movement of love toward God. If it deepens an individual's love of God or increases interior peace, that would be a favorable sign. If it fails to deepen love or causes agitation, it should be critically examined or set aside. These simple tests have a remarkable effectiveness. Sometimes the authenticity of impulses can be glaringly apparent when so examined. For example, if a certain impulse seems to wither when we compare it to an inner act of love toward God, it should probably be dismissed. It may also help to test impulses by time. Sometimes by postponing a decision for a day or even for several hours, the impulse may seem, for example, less attractive.

There are also exterior tests for an impulse or leading. It should be rationally examined in light of its consequences. After consideration, for example, it may seem clear that the results of a given leading would be improper. Or something which might deeply trouble another person should be suspected. Any leading which contradicts God's law should, of course, be rejected out of hand. It is not impossible that God may lead an individual in ways contrary to these rough norms, but such cases deserve very serious consideration and probably consultation with mature and prudent Christians who have a deep interior life. For instance, it is conceivable that God may ask an individual to do something causing inner turmoil for a while or upsetting to others. But in these cases, where the leading is genuine, peace will follow and the action will be in accord with charity.

It is also possible for an individual to act upon an authentic leading in an inappropriate manner. Not all leadings are accompanied by a revealed plan to implement them. Frequently individuals confuse their own idea of how to carry out a leading with the leading itself, and this can result in great confusion. For example,

God may lead an individual to seek reconciliation with another person. If that individual does so, however, in an impulsive or dramatic and offensive manner, he may have confused the authentic leading itself with the first idea which came into his mind about how to respond to it. It is necessary to seek to understand the meaning of the leading and to then seek to understand an appropriate means to carry it out.

Absolute certainty about a leading is not necessary. It is, in fact, rare and may result from an ill-founded over-confidence. A reasonable critical examination is sufficient to test most leadings. If, after an appropriate period of prayerful and thoughtful reflection, a leading continues to appear good, it can be humbly followed in most cases. The extent of an examination, of course, should be proportionate to the seriousness of the leading. A leading to quit work and become a hermit, for example, requires much more elaborate testing than an impulse to speak out at a prayer meeting.

Some may assume that the leadings of the Spirit are ordered exclusively toward exterior action or deeds. Such an assumption overlooks one of the most important aspects of the leadings of the Spirit. The work of the Spirit is, above all, to lead one to Jesus. The object of many of the Spirit's leadings is to draw us to interior attitudes which please God and to interior acts of contrition, humility, patience or love. For example, the promptings of the Spirit can serve to draw attention from the day's business in order to evoke a simple and brief act of love for God. Or one may be moved by the Spirit in compassion or cheerfulness toward another. These interior leadings are a very important part of the Spirit's work and should receive prompt attention.

The leadings of the Spirit, then, are an important facet of God's work. They should be welcomed by a Christian. They provide a means by which God's will can be known more completely. They should not be met with indifference or regarded as a source of trouble, but treated as a better means of loving God. While seeking to be led in whatever way God wishes, it is a mistake to be overly impressed with spiritual leadings. The best advice one might give is to seek to be led and mistrust leadings. Understood properly, this advice is important for a balanced charismatic Christianity.

C. Seeking God's Will

Throughout one's life, there are a variety of choices which must be made. Each of them has some impact on one's life and some effect on other decisions. For example, the choice of a job or a neighborhood has certain consequences. Although leadings of the Spirit can be a factor in these matters, it is necessary to recognize that God guides men in more natural and ordinary channels as well. These choices come upon a person in various ways. Some are forced by outside circumstances, some by the passing of time, and some by personal choice. They are not at all beyond God's interest or concern, and it is important to learn prayerfully to seek his guidance in making them.

There are, of course, levels of importance. Some decisions will have long-range effects. Such decisions as the choice of a spouse and a career are examples. An intermediate level involves issues of lesser impact which are still substantial. They could include taking a particular job, going to college, or moving to a given location. There is also an immediate level such as whether to do something today or how to spend this afternoon. These distinctions are vague and overlap but they do indicate relative levels of importance.

1. Priorities and Levels

One factor in seeking guidance involves ordering priorities. Levels of importance affect priorities. A long-range decision such as a career choice should influence intermediate and immediate actions. If a long-range decision is prayerfully made and entrusted to God, more immediate actions which would contradict it do not make sense. For example, a decision to do something that would jeopardize one's family life runs counter to the decision, already ratified by God, to be married. Such a decision cannot be reasonably entertained.

Important decisions made before an individual consciously became concerned about guidance should not be despised. God guides men through their lives whether they recognize his presence or not. He brings good out of every situation and can turn a poor choice into a wonderful opportunity. In most cases, the major commitments an individual has made are valid. They set the stage, as it were, for a life of grace. There is a dangerous tendency to imagine an ideal set of circumstances. It must be recognized, though, that no situation is perfect. For example, an individual having received the charismatic experience may dream of freedom from job and home to work "full-time" for the Lord. Many pastors will testify, however, that working "full-time" for the Lord is not a dream. It is necessary to recognize that the setting of a life does not matter so much as an individual's response to God in that setting. It is by seeking to grow in love and grace in the circumstances in which we are situated that we will grow closer to God.

After receiving the charismatic experience, though, it may be valuable to reconsider some commitments and perhaps even major ones. This can be done in a prudent manner. Generally those who are awakened spiritually after having already made major lifetime commitments to family, home, life style, and career have here the framework in which they must work out their salvation. Adjustments normally will be minor. It is important for such individuals to resist the temptation to daydream unrealistically of so-called greener pastures. In the unusual event that God is calling for a basic change of framework, that call will gradually become manifest to all concerned not as a threat but as a gesture of love which can be cheerfully embraced.

All too often, Christians who are concerned about guidance think only in terms of matters on which they have sensed explicit leadings. However, God's guidance is operative whether or not it is apparent to us. He guides all who entrust themselves to him. Cooperation is important, but it need not always be explicit. It is not necessary, for example, that a child understand every aspect of his parents' actions. Parents can care for him without his understanding, and there are times when he will not realize what they are doing. In the same sense, God has a basic care for each of his people. It is important to accept this care cheerfully and to believe in his guidance in the circumstances of our life. It is important to cultivate a fundamental trust in his goodness which does not demand to be "in" on each and every decision.

Where major decisions are yet to be made in life, they should be made prayerfully. It is not wrong to actively seek leadings, but it is foolish to obey the leadings thus sought without going through a process of discernment. Where God wishes to lead strongly, he is quite capable of so doing. Christians do not need to be afraid of testing leadings critically. Younger people generally have made fewer lifelong commitments. As they make them, they can be assured of God's guidance. Normally they will be accompanied by some anxiety and even misgivings. If they are undertaken in loyalty to God, it is not possible to make a serious mistake.

2. External Factors

There are objective means by which a Christian can know God's will as well. They include revelation, the teaching of the Church, natural law, civil law, and common sense. Taken as a whole, these factors offer some broad and objective criteria by which a decision can be examined. They provide an insight into God's workings which balances personal and subjective considerations in a healthy way. In seeking guidance, a person should seriously consult them.

Sometimes they offer absolute rules for various decisions or problems. For example, God could not lead an individual to commit an immoral action. In a given situation, affection and passion may distort an individual's judgment. Morality, revelation, and the teaching of the Church, however, make God's will clear. More often they shed light on particular issues. Although they do not offer hard and fast answers, they point in a general direction and suggest some boundaries within which an answer must fall. For instance, marriage is sacred in God's eyes, and anything which mortally destroys or harms marriage such as adultery would clearly be wrong. But other activities must also be considered in light of their effect on the marriage and family. For example, an activity which is good and proper in itself would have to be carefully reconsidered if it serves to seriously weaken the family. God's will regarding marriage is expressed in a negative command. It follows, though, that his will embraces the positive. It can be concluded that it is his will that marriages be built up. There is no need for a special revelation regarding factors such as these. God has already made his wishes about them quite clear.

3. Knowing God's Will

Knowing God's will requires more than an ability to sense leadings or sort out options. Both of these activities are mechanical. It is one thing to sense leadings and quite another to act upon them in a wise manner. A deeper expertise than a mere technical ability is needed to understand and make decisions and choices in accord with God's will. Neither a computer nor a balance sheet for pro's and con's will suffice. What is necessary is an intricate process involving mind and heart. Being led by the Spirit does not exempt a person from thinking. Our mind can help us understand the will of God. Minds renewed in Christ are able to approach issues with great clarity and vigor. The heart has an important role in this process, too. It can sometimes go to the essence of a complicated question long before the mind is able to sort it out.

We are really talking about the need for wisdom. Wisdom is not a virtue easily or speedily acquired. It requires time and patience for minds and hearts to grow in understanding the paths which lead to God, but every Christian is capable of such growth and must work toward it. This wisdom, as Solomon says, is a precious gift outweighing all others, and it is earnestly to be sought. Intelligence has little bearing upon this process. In regard to knowing God's will, the intelligent and the unintelligent are equal in God's eyes. The one who is competent in matters concerning God's will is the one whose heart moves promptly and generously to please him. This is an interior state in which men are led almost intuitively after a while by the love of God. This wisdom is sometimes briefly experienced when a person receives the charismatic experience.

Such wisdom can be cultivated. Sports provide us with an excellent analogy. Athletes who are experts can react instinctively or, one might say, intuitively in a given situation. In football, a good quarterback can take advantage of an unexpected opportunity for a gain. In such situations, the player "thinks on his feet" since there is no time for reflection. Body and mind seem to be united in simultaneous movement. Such situations may appear to an observer to be a matter of luck. In fact, the player is an expert or, one might say, an artist who has labored long and hard. He brings a combination of mental alertness, experience, an excellent physique and discipline together. Intuitive knowledge is possible in a relationship as well. It can often be seen in marriage. When two people share their lives for a long time, they come to know one another by second nature. They can almost read each other's mind. They are able to sense each other's needs and desires and, if they have disciplined themselves in love, are quick to anticipate them. Such a relationship is possible, too, with God. It is, in fact, in the context of such a relationship that Christians come to discern the leadings of the Spirit. As one grows in docility and love, cultivating the close familiarity which comes from a life of prayer, the process will be a quick movement of mind and heart in an act of love. The wise man will intuitively pick the right path toward God. God's love within will disclose the way.

The fact that this is a process of trial and error should not be discouraging, nor should the fact that we may at times become fools for Christ. Charismatics are not exempt from the normal processes of growth. They do, however, have great consolation during this time in their experience of the Holy Spirit. He is guide and comforter during these times.

Christians must be guided by a combination of common sense which enables them to keep their feet on the ground and faith which enables them to behold Jesus. As they grow familiar with the ways of God, they will come to recognize the gentle tug by which God will often seek to draw the heart to him in love. This subtle movement will become a sure guide. Many years and much experience are necessary before one arrives at this simple way of love. It takes much listening to learn to hear the shepherd's voice and distinguish it amid the babel of noises that make up life. It is a love which takes delight in the Beloved and in pleasing him by every movement of heart and mind. In knowing God's will, it is not necessary to have a totally firm or certain conviction about a given course. It is enough to have prayerfully and seriously considered a decision and to have made it in love. God is more pleased by the virtues of faith, hope, and love in our heart than by complete certainty about the course undertaken. Furthermore, as our choices more perfectly express our love of God, they will not be far wrong.

D. Making a Decision

A person's life is filled with decisions. A Christian wants them to be in accord with God's will and to be guided by God in making them. The fact that God does lead and guide, however, does not exempt us from having to work them through except in very rare instances. It may, therefore, be of some help to examine the process involved in making a decision. Such an undertaking is necessarily of limited value because decisions vary in importance and the opportunities for reflections differ. Furthermore, the involvement of others adds another set of factors. Nevertheless, there is some benefit in attempting a brief analysis of the process by which a decision is made.

We will consider the process in three stages: deliberation, choice, and action.

1. Deliberation

This is the stage at which we gather data. A person should earnestly seek the truth and God's will above everything.

a. It is important for an individual to attempt to understand what he wants and why. Sometimes Christians will simply say: "I want God's will." But it is important to understand one's own will before being able to discern God's will. At the outset, an individual should try to determine the course of action he favors, if any.

b. It is necessary to face the truth about our motives. Often we seek to deceive ourselves and hide real motives which may be unacceptable behind other motives which are more acceptable. It is possible, for example, to allow the common good or the interest of others to cloak the fact that we are acting for selfish personal benefit. It is important to seek to uncover our raw motives in the clear light of charity. When there is a complex series of interlocking motives, we should try to sort through them and determine the primary motives.

c. It is valuable to consider the courses of action available. Various advantages and disadvantages attached to each should be noted. It may help to list them in writing. The factors which we must weigh include responsibilities, anything relevant from the objective order such as the moral law or the teaching of the Church, principles which may apply, signs, leadings from God, promptings, the opinions of others, and the consequences of the decision.

d. The essential question to be asked is: "What is God's will?" If a person seeks to serve God, God's interests must come first. In the long run, of course, the interests coincide, but it does not always appear so. Often there seems to be a choice between our own will and God's. A Christian should always seek to act in the way most pleasing to God. Every action should spring from a living faith and love for his will. A person should work to make pleasing God his principal motive.

Advantages and obstacles should be considered in light of God's will. God's will is a paramount consideration, whatever it may entail, and so obstacles or objections in themselves are not necessarily signs that a given course is wrong. These factors need to be considered and weighed but should be subordinate to the will of God. It is his will which is to be sought through this process, not the path of least resistance or the course which the world would deem most prudent.

e. It is necessary to weigh a given decision in the context of our life. It may be that another decision previously made, something that has happened, or the revealed Word of God can give direction in regard to this decision. If so, the implications of past choices should be considered.

f. In the process of deliberation, prayer has a vital place. Prayer in this sense should not be confused with seeking signs or leadings. They can be sought and must be treated as another factor to be weighed at this stage. In this case prayer means asking God to help by whatever means he chooses. The answer to this kind of prayer will rarely be dramatic, but, in a hidden and gentle way, God will draw our hearts toward the proper course.

g. Hardening into a course of action at the beginning of this stage should be avoided. This stage should be an open quest for the proper course of action. At times, however, people have already made up their minds and seek to justify the decision. Instead of sincerely seeking what is best through a free and prayerful process, we have settled the matter. It may be that the decision is the best, but it is foolish to deceive ourselves and others by pretending to be open-minded.

h. This process often is accompanied by a certain anxiety.

This may be a sign that we are not totally immersed in the Spirit but should not itself be a cause of anxiety. Although God can take anxieties away, he often does not. They can teach us humility and cause us to turn to him more fruitfully. However important a given decision may be, there is a more important lesson to be learned from it. Even the best decision is limited and after a while even the best solutions must be reconsidered. All decisions are frail and weak. Making decisions can lead us to the understanding that in God there is a stability beyond the change of time. Any decision made in truth and love can lead to an insight into this aspect of God's nature, and anxiety can often force us to look beyond the present toward eternity.

A fundamental belief lies behind this approach to decision-making. It is the conviction that God does not care as much about a decision as he does about the spirit in which it is made. He does not often show his will with absolute certainty. Such certainty is suspect. Rather, he lets us decide with glimpses and leadings, for he wants us to do his will spontaneously because we want to. It is by conforming our will to his will and by disciplining ourselves to seek him in all things that we grow in God's will. Such a process is not mechanical or magic but a process of love and growth.

2. Choice

In making a decision there comes a time to decide. A reasonable amount of time should be taken to consider the decision, but it is important to avoid procrastination or escape from the decision. There is a way of waiting for God's leadings which is false to God and is infantile. By so doing, a person simply waits until something appears to fall from heaven or until events decide the matter. This approach has nothing to do with seeking God's will. A decision has in fact been made here to do nothing, but it was not made for the love of God. It may be that God's will is that nothing be done, but, if so, the decision not to act should deliberately be made through this process and consecrated to God.

Understanding God's will is of course important in making a choice. In most cases, God's will is not identical with any option. It will be necessary to try to understand God's will and then determine which possible course of action best accomplishes it. The actual choice of a course of action may occur instantly or over a gradual period of time. How or when a choice is made will vary considerably, but, once made, it should be stated as clearly and explicitly as possible. It may help to formulate the decision in words and perhaps even to commit it to writing. It can also help to share it with others.

3. Action

Having made a decision, it must be commended to God and pursued with all one's strength. If it has been prayerfully made, God will honor it. Even if the course he might have preferred was not chosen, he honors decisions that men make and takes them into account. There should be no servile fear of God which paralyzes Christians for fear of making mistakes. If we sincerely seek to serve God, he will perfect us through our very mistakes. We need have no fear of him. For example, although God did not want Israel to have a king, they decided to choose one. God fitted their choice into his plan for their salvation in a most marvelous way. Although he was against it, he took them so seriously that his only Son came from the line of the royal family. In a similar manner, God can take a Christian's decisions and incorporate them into his plan.

And so, once a decision is made, it should be wholeheartedly embraced for the love of God and pursued as if it were his spoken command. It can be a prayer or offering of love to God. Of course, it is proper to test a decision, but not in such a way as to undermine our will to act. Obstacles are always encountered and their presence should not convince us that we have made the wrong decision. Obstacles test determination. A decision made in prayer and in faith can become a fortress against doubts and obstacles. When our decisions are under attack, it is important to summon up faith in a decision and to persevere in it. Throughout this entire process a person can rest secure in God's fundamental and all-embracing love. He will not permit fatal mistakes. When an individual is on the wrong track, he will erect impossible obstacles. When it is apparent that a decision cannot be carried out for external reasons, the impasse should be gracefully accepted, trusting in God's providence. The decision should then be prayerfully reconsidered. It may be a time to wait or to persevere, or it may be that God is calling for a change of plans. Although it may take time to understand these things, his gracious will and steadfast love will shepherd us.

V
Charismatic Gifts

It is the role of the Holy Spirit to quicken the entire body of Christ and to empower its various members. The Spirit's indwelling presence is, of course, the principal means by which this is accomplished. The Spirit also bestows special gifts which aid the Christian in his vocation.

Every baptized Christian has a use for the gifts of the Spirit. As members of Christ's body, all are called to exercise a function which the gifts can facilitate. In fact many Christians are unaware of their role in the body of Christ and cannot conceive of the value of spiritual gifts to assist them in this role. They are, as it were, asleep. The charismatic experience has served to bring many individuals to a living awareness of their role in the body of Christ and has made them aware of the various gifts of the Spirit given to assist them in this role.

The charismatic gifts are popularly recognized as a trademark of the charismatic renewal. There is much justification in this identification. Charismatics seek and exhibit the special gifts of the Spirit with an intensity and frequency rarely paralleled in the life of the Church. In any age, claimed supernatural manifestations such as speaking in unlearned languages, prophecy, miracles, and healings would attract attention. The gifts, at least the most unusual of them, attract attention to themselves. Despite this impression, these gifts are not identical with the charismatic movement or the charismatic experience of the Holy Spirit, nor do they represent its most important aspect. They do, however, represent an integral element of the renewal and one which has great significance for a new charismatic.

The charismatic gifts are special gifts of a preternatural nature given by the Spirit for the upbuilding of the body. This specialized use of the term "charismatic" is not identical to the popular usage which would label any attractive or magnetic personality "charismatic." Here it is used not to describe a person but to identify extraordinary gifts given by God in a manner differing from his bestowal of natural talents—though often complementing them —for the upbuilding of the Church.

The charismatic gifts are intrinsic to the Church. They are not an afterthought on God's part or a non-functional decoration. They represent a mode of operation which God uses to work in the Church. These gifts were operative and recognized in the early Church. Our Lord himself exercised many charismatic gifts, such as healing, discernment of spirits, the working of miracles, and amazing powers of teaching and preaching. Furthermore, he promised that such powers would accompany his disciples. During his own ministry, he conferred these powers upon the disciples, sending them out to heal and giving them power over demons (Lk. 9:1-2). He promised: "He who believes in me will also do the work that I do; and greater works than these will he do, because I go to the Father" (Jn. 14:12). The end of Mark's Gospel records the early Church's belief in Jesus' promise: "These signs will accompany those who believe: in my name they will cast out demons; they will speak in tongues; they will pick up serpents, and if they drink any deadly thing, it will not hurt them; they will lay their hands on the sick and they will recover" (Mk. 16:17-18). Acts chronicles the early Church's experience of the charismatic gifts. Miracles, prophecy, empowered preaching, healing, and the gift of tongues were a regular part of the life of the Church. In the Epistles, regular mention is made of the charismatic gifts in a fashion which indicates that their presence was normal (1 Thes. 1:5; 1 Cor. 2:4; 1 Cor. 12-14; 2 Cor. 12:1-4; Gal. 3:2-5). After the apostolic age, the exercise of these gifts diminished to a considerable extent but did not disappear. Church history offers considerable testimony to the function of the charismatic gifts in the lives of the saints. Recent examples of charismatic activity would include the ministry of the Curé of Ars, Padre Pio, and the healings at Lourdes. Nonetheless, charismatic activity has not been as common or as frequent as in the early Church. This fact, coupled with the recent reappearance of these gifts in plentitude, has given rise to an entire spectrum of theories which attempt to account for this interlude. As might be expected, some attribute the absence of such gifts to the absence of the Spirit, a disconcerting notion in light of the unequivocal promises of Christ. Others find in it fuel for anti-establishment or anti-hierarchical theories. More plausible theories point to a pristine age followed by centuries during which the Church grew into the fullness promised by Christ which was foreshadowed by the early Church. In seeking to explain the relative absence of the gifts, however, it must be recognized that these gifts were never entirely absent from the Church at any time and that the presence of the Spirit in the Church cannot be measured by the quantity of charismatic gifts exercised.

The teaching of Vatican II is of special value with regard to the gifts. The Council expressly recognizes the place of the charisms in the Church and the Christian life and cautiously encourages them. This teaching, in a certain sense, paved the way among Catholics for the acceptance of these gifts as manifested in the charismatic renewal and served considerably to quiet suspicion and hostility which might have resulted on several occasions in their suppression. From its outset, the charismatic movement has been marked by the presence of extraordinary workings of the Spirit. Extensive charismatic activity can also be traced to the holiness movements which preceded it. Among Pentecostals, charismatic activity was so common that the exercise of the gift of tongues became dogmatically identified with the reception of the gifts of Spirit. In the movement in the established churches the gifts have retained their vigor while being dissociated from such a crippling theology. The exercise of the charismatic gifts is a regular and important part of the charismatic renewal.

Scripture does not offer a systematic teaching on the charismatic gifts. Rather it treats them in a practical and specific fashion at times, and in a vague and general fashion at other times. St. Thomas Aquinas gave a lengthy treatment to the charisms, but later theology neglected them. Only recently have modern theologians begun to pay attention to their place in the Christian life. As a result, they can only be treated in a tentative way.

Because of the importance of the charismatic gifts, there is abroad in the renewal a moderately sized body of teaching of varying quality about the gifts and their uses. Some of it cites the scriptural texts in a way which lends an authority from Scripture which the texts themselves do not warrant. This teaching really flows from experience and reads its conclusions into Scripture. This is not to say that teaching based on experience may not be valid in whole or part, nor does it discount the value of using Scripture as a teaching tool. But it does say that Scripture can be used as an undisputed authority for a very limited number of points regarding the charismatic gifts, and teaching about the gifts which relies on Scripture often reads its conclusions into the cited text. In this chapter we will attempt to formulate some conclusions about the charisms, drawing on Scripture, the teaching of the Church, and contemporary experience.

1. The Source and Purpose of the Gifts

The source and purpose of the charismatic gifts are clear. Their source is Jesus who has poured out his Spirit. The gifts are authentic when they testify to his Lordship (1 Cor. 12:3; 1 Jn. 4:2), and however diverse they may be, it is the Spirit who is at work in every manifestation (1 Cor. 12:4-6). Their purpose is the upbuilding of the Church. This can be seen in the references to the gifts in 1 Corinthians. Paul lays down a general principle for the use of gifts in the assembly: "Let all things be done for edification" (1 Cor. 14:26). The gifts to which Paul refers—tongues, interpretation, knowledge and teaching—and presumably all other gifts exercised in the assembly were to further the purpose of the assembly. Specifically they were to instruct the listeners. They are valuable insofar as they contribute to this purpose. The person "who prophesies is greater than he who speaks in tongues" because intelligible messages instruct and edify whereas unintelligible ones do not. He also says: "I thank God that I speak in tongues more than you all; nevertheless, in church I would rather speak five words with my mind, in order to instruct others, than ten thousand words in a tongue" (1 Cor. 14:18-19). When they are abused, as in Corinth, Paul does not hesitate to spell out rules to insure that the gifts do edify. He limits tongue-speaking, for example, and requires an interpretation. He also proposes rules for the exercise of prophecy (1

Cor. 14:27-33). When the gifts build the church in its assembly, they are useful; when they do not, they should not be exercised.

It is reasonable to assume that the gifts were exercised on other occasions than when the church was assembled. Paul makes this clear in referring to his own use of tongues. He claims to speak in tongues more than any of the Corinthians, yet he does not seem to have used this gift in the assembly. He exercised, we may conclude, the gift outside of the assembly and, since "he who speaks in tongues edifies himself" (1 Cor. 14:4), presumably in private. The catalogue of gifts in 1 Corinthians as well as the one in Romans lists gifts whose use was probably not confined to the assembly such as healing, miracles (1 Cor. 12:9-10), service, contributions, aid, and acts of mercy (Rom. 12:7-8). The gifts referred to in Ephesians are ministries for the Church which were exercised at other times than when the Church was assembled. 1 Peter, in speaking of rendering service "by the strength which God supplies," seems to imply more than service at a liturgical rite (1 Pt. 4:11). In Acts the exercise of gifts outside of the assembly also can be observed. Peter and John heal the lame man at the gate of the temple (Acts 3:2) in response to a request for alms. Acts records that "many signs and wonders were done among the people by the hand of the apostles," so much so "that they even carried out the sick into the streets and laid them on beds and pallets, that as Peter came by at least his shadow might fall on some of them" (Acts 5:12, 15). Philip drew attention to himself in Samaria by his words and the signs which he did. He cast out spirits and healed some who were lame or paralyzed (Acts 8:6-7). Peter raised Tabitha from the dead at Joppa (Acts 9:36-43). Paul, too, worked miracles; he blinded Elymas the magician on Cyprus (Acts 13:4-12); at Iconium, there were "signs and wonders" (Acts 14:3); at Thyatira, he cast out an evil spirit from a soothsayer (Acts 16:16-18). At Ephesus "God did extraordinary miracles by the hands of Paul, so that handkerchiefs or aprons were carried away from his body to the sick, and diseases left them and the evil spirits came out of them" (Acts 19:11-12). At Troas, Paul raised Eutychus from the dead (Acts 20:7-12); Agabus prophesied at Ptolemais regarding Paul's imprisonment (Acts 21:10-11); on Malta, Paul was not harmed by a deadly viper's sting (Acts 28:3-6); he also cured many on Malta (Acts 28:7-10).

In these accounts the gifts further Christ's work, as when they strengthen and encourage an individual to assist him in his work for Christ. They are also for the benefit of believers, as in the case of Eutychus and Tabitha who were restored to health. Frequently, however, the exercise of the gifts is for non-believers. Many of the examples mentioned above drew non-Christians to acts of faith. In the assembly, too, they served this purpose. Paul speaks of the use of the gifts for the sake of the non-believers (1 Cor. 14:23-25).

The use of the gifts, then, can be understood in three ways: for believers in the assembly, for believers outside the assembly, and for non-believers. Each manner of use contributed to building the body. By instructing the assembly, by assisting a believer, or by drawing non-Christians to the faith the Church was built up.

These observations yield a valid principle for understanding the purpose of the gifts which can be used in regard to the contemporary charismatic movement. The gifts should be used to build up the Church. They are given for that purpose alone. They are meant to glorify Christ and draw attention to the power of God. They are not meant for private gain or personal glory. At assemblies, for example, their use should be orderly and contribute to the purpose of the assembly. In using a gift for the benefit of a Christian, there must be no thought of personal gain or advantage. In regard to their use in converting unbelievers, the Christian's conduct must be proper so as not to give undue occasion for scandal or hostility.

2. Classifying the Gifts

The gifts cannot be classified with great precision. Scripture mixes gifts and ministries and offers little insight into the meaning of the various lists it contains. At the beginning of Chapter 12 in 1 Corinthians, for example, St. Paul lists gifts, and at the end of the same chapter he lists ministries. Some of these ministries are named for the exercise of a gift such as healing or speaking in tongues while others seemingly have no relationship to the gifts previously listed. In Ephesians the ministries for the church are referred to as gifts. The casual presentation of these gifts in Scripture strongly indicates that Paul was hardly offering a systematic treatise on the gifts. The lists presented appear to be a rough inventory in which some gifts were considered in themselves while others were thought of as embodied in ministries. Attempts to try to specifically understand each gift in Paul's list, like knowledge or wisdom, and to formulate treatises on them have generally been unsuccessful.

Contemporary experience serves to reinforce the opinion that gifts are not easily classified. Some seem to be regularly exercised, such as tongues or prophecy, while others, such as miracles, are less so. In addition, some individuals could be said to have a regular exercise of a gift, so much so as to warrant calling it a ministry, while others may have a ministry but infrequently exercise a charismatic gift. Furthermore, it is difficult to distinguish at times between natural abilities and charismatic gifts. At what point, for example, is it the case that a naturally gifted speaker exercises a charismatic gift of inspired preaching? In a broader sense, the Spirit works in extraordinary ways when necessary in the work of the Church. Every priest, for instance, will admit to times when he said things that seemed to be from God in a much more direct manner than usual in administering the sacrament of penance. Many Christians, too, will recognize a certain inspiration or facility at times when counsel or consolation is needed. There is little sense, I believe, in expending much energy in seeking to create a rigid or overly-sophisticated category of gifts and ministries. For example, it is foolish for members of a newly-formed group to decide who has what gifts and to designate ministries on that basis. The gifts change, as do the circumstances in which they are to be used. Furthermore, they grow and develop. It is one thing to suggest a label for a gift which is budding in a person, and quite another to have a rigid system into which that gift must fit. Such an approach is liable to do violence to the unique and extraordinary character of the gifts. Rather than identifying a gift with precision or clearly marking the line between charism and natural ability, charismatics should be encouraged to concentrate upon works in which their efforts seem to bear fruit. In these areas they should seek to be open to the Spirit's leadings in whatever way they are given. Other than this, hard and fast conclusions about the gifts and their use—especially when applied to a particular person—when based on limited experience of a few years' duration should be avoided.

Because some theoretical framework is helpful in speaking of the gifts, I would suggest a flexible classification: tongues, word gifts, and miraculous gifts. Tongues exists in a category of its own. Its principal use is private and so only indirectly builds up the Church. The word gifts seem to form a category which is related. Prophecy, tongues with interpretation, inspired preaching, and inspired teaching fall into this category. The miraculous gifts are different from the word gifts and also form a related category. Even these distinctions, however, blend in individual cases or situations.

3. Possible Abuses

The reason that St. Paul wrote to the Corinthians about the charismatic gifts was to correct their abuse. From his letter we can infer that tongues and prophecy were being improperly used by the Corinthian assembly. Not only can they be misused, but their use is no indication that the gifts are of benefit to anyone. Excessive manifestations of prophecy among the Corinthians simply meant to St. Paul that no one was able to reflect on what was said. Nor was the abundance of gifts in the Corinthian community a sign of the maturity of that community. Paul told them that they were babes because there were quarrels and divisions among them. It can also be concluded that the mere exercise of a gift is no test of its validity; every gift must be weighed and tested. Neither is the fact that a person can exercise a gift any indication of his or her holiness or maturity.

As we reflect upon the limitations to which these gifts are subject, it becomes readily apparent that they are susceptible to misuse and even abuse as well as misunderstanding. Unlike deeper workings of the Spirit such as patience or charity, they are not signs of growth in perfection nor do they perfect us in a supernatural way. They can, however, be an occasion for growth in holiness, and a new charismatic should be concerned to see that such growth follows their use. This kind of proficiency requires hard work as well as wisdom. For this reason, growth in technical proficiency in the use of the gifts must be distinguished from a growth in charity in their use. At this point we are not so much concerned with technique—how to recognize and use the gifts more effectively—although that is important. Rather, we are concerned here with emphasizing the fact that even technical perfection in the use of the gifts does not mean charity or holiness on the part of the person using them or for whom they are used. There is necessary, then, a recognition that there is an additional dimension to be taken into account in the exercise of the gifts and that failure to consider it will result in abuse of the gifts.

Healing offers a good example because it is so spectacular and important. Healing ministries can be powerful yet lacking in the dimension of which we speak. For instance, a great healer can be under such pressure as to be driven to excessive use of alcohol or to illicit sex. The healings may be valid, but something clearly is missing in its exercise which may ultimately discredit the ministry. Or the people who see the healings may be impressed in the wrong way and fix their attention upon the healer rather than Christ.

Many of the abuses to which the gifts are subject can be avoided through the cultivation of a sound and healthy attitude toward them. It is especially important to avoid touting their sensational aspects and to be leary of over-emotional scenes. Of course, by their very nature some of the gifts attract attention and arouse an emotional response. But where there is a deliberate manipulation of emotions through various effects in order to stir them up or an overplay of the dramatic element, there is grave danger of emphasizing mistaken attitudes. The cult of the sensational is easily awakened, and once awakened it is not soon put to rest. We are all susceptible to a morbid curiosity for the supernatural (preternatural, really), and this curiosity is not satisfied but only grows by meeting it.

A healthy attitude toward the gifts is one which is basically positive toward them while seeking to avoid potential abuses. For example, such an attitude would honor the one who loves more than the one who heals if the latter does not love as well. And it would honor the healer much more for his love and goodness than for his gift of healing. It would emphasize the spiritual healing of mind and spirit much more than physical healing, recognizing that even one who has been healed will die someday. The importance of self-control should also be recognized. The gifts are not ecstatic. The person who exercises a gift has control over it. He or she can choose whether or not to speak in tongues, prophesy or interpret, for example. Paul insists, in writing to the Corinthians, that "the spirits of prophets are subject to prophets" (1 Cor. 14:32). In a negative vein, excessive emotional displays should be avoided. They can easily distort the work which God is trying to accomplish. Outbursts or antics should be regarded suspiciously and privately questioned in a peaceful and prudent manner. A cult of personality around a charismatic, such as a healer, is a special danger. In actual practice, it is hard to refrain from identifying the gift with the one who exercises it. Scripture even records instances where miracle workers were treated as Gods. Such adulation, however, must be severely discouraged by those who have these gifts and by their friends for the good of the individual who exercises the gift—since pride is such a deadly sin—and for the good of the charismatic movement. Like Paul, they must loudly and repeatedly insist: "We also are men, of like nature with you" (Acts 14:15).

The recognition of the possible abuses which can result from the exercise of the gift requires more than indifference on the part of some toward a yet unrealized danger and negativism on the part of a few others. It calls for a balanced and affirmative emphasis of a healthy attitude toward the gifts, their role in the Christian life, and the people who exercise them. Unhealthy tendencies must be resisted if the gifts are to find their proper place in the life of the whole Church. Short-sighted emphasis of the attention-getting in the gifts will have the long-run effect of discrediting their use for the majority of Christians. In all of this, our Lord's own cautious and careful attitude to the miraculous should be our guide. In Christian communities the gifts have a working role, and those who exercise them are workers. Those who exercise the "plainer" gifts are no less important than those whose gifts are spectacular. The administrator is as important as the healer for the upbuilding of the body. A gift is a call to service, not a badge of honor. It is like being handed a hammer and being told to build!

4. Authority and the Gifts

The gifts and those who exercise them are subject to authority which can regulate their use and judge their validity. Paul did not hesitate to prescribe particular and somewhat arbitrary rules for the Corinthians. He set numerical limits for those who were to speak in tongues or to prophesy (1 Cor. 14:27-29). He insisted that they "test everything," implying especially prophecy to which he had just referred. He insisted on obedience to his instructions, telling the Corinthians: "If anyone thinks that he is a prophet, or spiritual, he should acknowledge that what I am writing to you is a command of the Lord. If anyone does not recognize this, he is not recognized" (1 Cor. 14:37-38).

Because the gifts are open to abuse either through sincere mistake or malice, their use requires regulation. Indeed, proper use of the gifts is only possible through leadership. In a prayer meeting, this principle is self-evident. A function of leadership is to encourage the proper use of the gifts. It is an interesting phenomenon that often where the gifts are used in an uncontrolled fashion, their use tends to die out, whereas in situations where they are subordinate to the good of the assembly and used in a calm and orderly fashion, they tend to grow in depth and importance. Common sense indicates that a group can benefit from only so many divine messages at a given time. If they are to be weighed seriously and not simply follow each other in senseless procession, there can only be a limited number. Beyond that, there is an overload. Regulation, in this sense, is healthy, and rather than quenching the Spirit, it insures its fullest manifestation. Those who exercise gifts must recognize this principle in the use of their gifts. Especially while visiting groups, charismatics must learn to use these gifts in an orderly manner consistent with the judgment of the leaders of the assembly.

This principle is more far reaching, however. If those in authority in a given situation are qualified to order the use of the charismatic gifts, those who exercise the apostolic authority within the Church are even more qualified to do so. Bishops, as shepherds of their flock, are called upon by virtue of their office to judge and order the working of the charismatic gifts. Vatican Council II insisted that those who use the gifts "must act in communion with their brothers in Christ, especially with their pastors. The latter must make a judgment about the true nature and proper use of these gifts, not in order to extinguish the Spirit, but to test all things and to hold fast to what is good" (*Decree on the Apostolate of the Laity*, n. 3). Charismatics must recognize this episcopal role and seek to receive it. Just as the Corinthians benefited from Paul's fatherly advice, charismatics can greatly benefit from the advice of their bishops and pastors. An often used argument contesting this role is that unless an individual has exercised a charismatic gift, he cannot judge it. That would be like saying that a doctor cannot diagnose an illness which he may not have had. Furthermore, it must be recognized that because the bishop has an office in the Church, there are available to him charismatic gifts which enable him to better fulfill his office. These gifts complement the sacrament of orders through which the Spirit works in a powerful way strengthening the episcopal ministry. To insist that a bishop be an expert or practitioner of particular charismatic gifts before being qualified to judge them reveals an absence of faith in the Spirit who apportions to each person the gifts necessary for his or her service.

5. Should Everyone Exercise a Gift Like Tongues?

In the charismatic renewal, the frequent occurrence of the charisms gives rise to the question of whether everyone should exercise a charismatic gift. There are some arguments for this position. Scripture does seem to indicate that the gifts were commonly experienced in the early Church. Charismatics today also commonly experience the gifts. Furthermore, theology has come to understand that the charismatic gifts are tools given to believers in their work of serving the Church. It seems reasonable to conclude that these gifts are given to all, since everyone is called to service in the Church. It must be recognized, though, that it is one thing to suggest that charisms are given to all and quite another to argue that everyone can and should receive a specific and manifest gift. Because this issue most frequently arises over the gift of tongues, it will be considered here. Scripture does not offer any light on which gift is given to whom. It does suggest that each individual does not have every gift, and Paul does pose the rhetorical question "Do all speak with tongues?" implying that they do not. He may, however, be referring here to their use in the assembly. Nevertheless, it is not possible to seriously maintain from Scripture that every person should receive a specific gift such as tongues.

It is true that tongues is a valuable gift especially for prayer and that everyone should be encouraged to be open to its exercise. To do so, however, by dogmatically maintaining the theory that all can and should receive the gift is very unwise. If a gift like tongues can be received by everyone, the burden of proof rests with the proponents of such a theory. Limited experience in charismatic circles is hardly sufficient to establish such a theory, and several leading charismatics continue to insist that despite their personal openness to the gift, they have not received it. Such statements cast serious doubt upon the validity of a universal thesis about tongues from the outset. This position, however, cannot be ruled out *a priori*, and those who favor it should defend it in the public forums of the charismatic renewal—theology, and related disciplines, and the Church. In the meantime, however, it is most unwise and unfair to base pastoral practice or teaching on such a disputed theory.

There is, of course, a practical problem which this theory conveniently solves. It is true that some people who could receive the gift of tongues are hesitant about it and need to be encouraged. Indeed, some actually would grasp at any excuse to avoid asking for the gift. By resolutely maintaining that all should receive tongues, it is possible to cut through such objections, often with good results. It must be recognized, however, that there are other means of encouraging these people or dealing with the problem besides advocating a blanket theory. In the first place, all should be encouraged to be open to receiving the charismatic gifts, and especially tongues. Furthermore, in some situations an individual should be specifically encouraged to pray out in tongues and perhaps receive various types of assistance, even though at times mistakes in judgment will occur and should be expected. It is far better to proceed with an open-minded attitude than to force individuals to receive a gift they may fear or to create feelings of guilt. The good will and sincerity of those seeking the gifts must always be presumed. It is even possible and surely is wrong to cause people to manifest a nonsense baby talk because of an underlying pressure to receive this gift. Such results do not glorify God, and they bring the authentic exercise and value of the gifts under suspicion. Where there is adequate appreciation of gifts like tongues and proper and balanced use of them, God will open individuals to accept them with little fuss or attention. It is hard to refuse a good thing, and in cases in which it is crucial for an individual to receive tongues or another gift, God can either give such discernment or create a situation in which the gift is received.

Charismatics will insure a much more happy reception of the gifts by allowing individuals to freely discover their worth and seek them under the inspirations of the Spirit rather than by promulgating a theory of the gifts which virtually makes them a necessary sign of openness to God's Spirit and the mark of a true charismatic.

The extent to which an individual should be encouraged to seek charismatic gifts is a moot question. He should be encouraged to form a positive attitude about them. Questions and misgivings should be addressed. If interested, he should be assisted in seeking the gifts. This assistance can be active and should be positive. What must be avoided, though, is a tone that makes the reception of any particular gift simply automatic and something everyone can exercise.

6. A Detailed Examination of Three Specific Gifts

Rather than treat each charismatic gift, we will focus on three specific gifts—tongues, prophecy, and healing. These gifts have been selected because they represent each general type of charismatic gift and because in themselves they are the object of much interest and controversy. Furthermore, they are the gifts to which someone entering the charismatic experience is most frequently exposed.

a. The Gift of Tongues

The gift of tongues is a charismatic gift in which an individual speaks aloud in an unlearned vocabulary. It is a gift referred to at the end of Mark's Gospel, in Paul's letters, and in Acts. Tongues has already been examined in regard to the question of whether everyone can speak in tongues. It is a gift commonly experienced among charismatics. There are some serious questions related to it such as whether it represents a genuine language. Some scholars have even argued that it was intended only for the early Church, while others assert that it originated in Oriental mystery cults despite Paul's sharp distinction (1 Cor. 12:2-3). It is, however, generally recognized that the gift of tongues as experienced in the charismatic renewal is a genuine gift of the Spirit. It attracts more sensational attention than it warrants. Despite popular conceptions, its exercise is quite plain, and at a prayer meeting tongues is often mistaken for quiet prayer in a known foreign language by visitors.

The primary purpose of tongues is to aid prayer. "One who speaks in a tongue speaks not to men but to God. . . . He utters mysteries in the Spirit" (1 Cor. 14:2). Tongues serves as a vehicle by which an individual can turn to God. It is not perhaps the most important form of prayer, but it is useful. It is of assistance in petition. At times when we are uncertain about how to pray for a particular intention, serious prayer in tongues can be of considerable value. A person can lift up his cause to God in an earnest manner through tongues. Its most valuable use, however, is in praise of God. Praise is a most important aspect of prayer and one which rarely comes naturally. For many, tongues has been the means by which they were introduced to prayers of praise. As they prayed in tongues, their hearts were elevated in worship of God. Gradually they begin to praise God in their native tongues and in silence. There are times when God's wonder and majesty call for a response beyond the ability of any language. Praise in tongues gives us a tongue, as it were, to proclaim his glory. Tongues is valuable in prayer because it partially occupies the mind, imagination, and body, thereby freeing a person to turn more deeply to God. It helps prevent distractions and enables a person to lift himself toward God in a more total manner. In this respect it is not dissimilar to the rosary.

Tongues is a gift which is commonly given, and it can be

sought through prayer. When it is first given, it may only be in the form of a few disjointed syllables, although it can come as a rich vocabulary. The experience of the gift is not necessarily consoling, and so it may seem disappointing at first. Through regular use, however, it will become apparent to an individual in short order whether the gift is authentic or illusory. In seeking the gift, it is important to be relaxed. The assistance of other Christians can be of considerable help. One should not be afraid to seek tongues. Oftentimes the desire for the gift comes from God himself who wishes an individual to seek it. It should, however, be sought peacefully and moderately.

Once received, tongues should be used regularly. The most appropriate use is in the daily prayer. At some point in a regular period of prayer, tongues may be valuable in praise or petition. It also can be of value throughout the day. At times it can be quietly used to set a tone of prayer. For example, when doing routine housework or when driving, prayer in tongues can dispose us toward God. At times it can be accompanied by spiritual consolations, while at other times it is not. It would be wrong to expect consolations regularly or to stop using the gift if consolations are not present. In fact, in times of dryness, prayer in tongues can be a great aid.

Tongues can also be used in the assembly. When it is spoken to the entire assembly, it should be interpreted. This use of tongues with interpretation resembles prophecy. There is another use of tongues quite common in charismatic gatherings known as a "word of prayer." During a word of prayer, an entire group will begin to pray aloud simultaneously, each in his or her own way. Many individuals will pray in tongues at this time and the word of prayer will often end with the group singing in tongues. Although this could seem to be an exercise in chaos, it is normally a beautiful and harmonious form of prayer. This manner of prayer does not violate the principle established by St. Paul for the Corinthians. It is not intended to instruct the assembly, but to be a common exercise of worship. Where it is done in an orderly fashion, it upbuilds the assembly.

Tongues, then, is a valuable gift of prayer. It is an important gift and should be sought and valued.

b. The Gift of Prophecy

Prophecy is a gift barely understood today. Its object is not to predict the future but to reveal God's Word. As such, it is consistent with the major strain of prophetic inspiration in the Old Testament and distinct from the ancient world's general understanding and use of divine communications.

The New Testament speaks of a prophetic revival. For several hundred years there had been no great prophets. Jesus was immediately preceded by John the Baptist who was the greatest of the prophets—and more than a prophet (cf. Lk. 2:36); Christ's birth was accompanied by a minor prophetic chorus through Zechariah (Lk. 1:67ff), Simeon (Lk. 7:25ff), and the prophetess Anna (Lk. 2:36). Furthermore, both Jesus and his disciples regarded his life and ministry as the fulfillment of the major prophecies of the Old Testament. On Pentecost, Peter announced the fulfillment of Joel's prophecy that all were to receive the gift of prophecy—even the servants (cf. Nm. 11:29). Prophecy was frequently exercised in the apostolic Church (Acts 11:27ff; 13:1; 19:6; 21:10ff; Eph. 4:11; 1 Tm. 1:18; 4:14; 1 Jn. 4:1). Paul refers to the gift of prophecy, ordering, for example, that it is not to be despised (1 Thes. 5:20; cf. 1 Cor. 12—14; Rom. 12:6).

Jesus, of course, is the prophet par excellence. He, above all, has come to reveal God's Word. He speaks for God in a direct way that the Old Testament prophets could not. He is the prophet predicted by Moses (Acts 3:22). The Church shares in Christ's prophetic ministry. The Church itself is prophetic and various ministries of prophecy exist in it. The gift of prophecy has not been common in the Church since its first centuries, although it has not been extinct, being evident, for instance, in the lives of several saints. Some scholars would argue, in fact, that the gift of prophecy was intended to disappear with the apostolic Church, being intended by God only for its initial flowering and rendered unnecessary later by Scripture and the teaching office of the Church. They lamely support this theory by citing Paul's statement in 1 Corinthians 13:8 that prophecy "will pass away," conveniently ignoring Paul's reference to knowledge in the same way. The value of knowledge has not yet passed away, and it is clear that in this passage Paul is referring to the end of time when prophecy and knowledge, both imperfect, will be supplanted by love which is perfect.

The reasons for the paucity of the gift of prophecy are not clear, for the theories which apply to the diminishment of the gifts apply to prophecy as well. Its value for the Church and its revival stands as perhaps the most important contribution which the charismatic renewal can make to the universal Church. Prophecy is a vital channel by which God speaks his Word to the Church. It complements and completes Scripture and the teaching office of the Church, though it is subordinate to them. Through the gift of prophecy, the Word of God is a living reality to the Church and Jesus can manifest himself to the Church in an immediate way.

Prophecy is an operation of the Spirit in which the Spirit's role might be termed active. He inspires. 2 Peter 1:21 states that "no prophecy ever came by the impulse of man, but men moved by the Holy Spirit spoke from God." Prophecy can be distinguished from an intellectual insight in which the intellect is stimulated by an outside force. In prophecy, the intellect is passive and the prophet cooperates by relating the inspiration which is given. St. Thomas describes the intellect in prophecy as "human intellect passive to the enlightening of the divine light."

It must be recognized, however, that the Spirit does work through the prophet's vocabulary and personality. The prophet's role in prophecy is important. For example, the message is given in the vocabulary of the prophet. Prophecy can be of mixed value depending upon the prophet. It is best to look to prophets with ministries tested over a period of time. Factors like nervousness, for example, could cause an inexperienced prophet to relate only part of the inspiration. Or the prophet may confuse something like interior passions or his own insights with the prophetic inspiration. Furthermore, in charismatic circles where prophecy is common, it is quite possible to confuse some other spiritual inspiration for the upbuilding of the group such as a vision or exhortation. Uncertain as to how to relate this inspiration, a person might express it in a prophetic mode. Such a message would be a "non-prophecy" rather than a false prophecy. In prophecy the speaker speaks for God in the first person. A person who has received an inspiration of another sort might be tempted to adopt the prophetic style because it is a mode accepted by the group as signifying a divine message. This practice should be strongly discouraged, however, because it is frequently apparent that the speaker is making the message fit the mode and it appears false. "Non-prophecy" can cast a bad light on authentic prophecy. It only takes slight effort and a little teaching to accustom a group to use other means besides the first-person prophetic style to communicate inspirations which are not prophecies.

Scripture speaks of both the gift of prophecy and the office of prophet in the Church. It is likely that each congregation had a number of individuals with the gift of prophecy who were recognized as prophets. In this technical sense, it is unlikely that everyone who ever exercised the gift of prophecy would have been called a prophet. In the charismatic renewal, this pattern also exists. Some individuals regularly exercise the gift of prophecy, and others do so only on occasion but with great effect. It is also the case that some individuals are given prophetic gifts for some situations—e.g., for a regular gathering—and not for others. It can be speculated with some degree of probability that should a widespread renewal of the gift of prophecy occur, it will be in a varied manner with differing levels of prophetic ministry. Generally, prophecy is valid only for a given group at a given time. Sometimes, though, a prophecy will pertain to that group with greater force than just for a passing moment. The same observation would hold true of private prophetic messages to individuals. It is reasonable to conclude that the exercise of the gift of prophecy could be relevant to the Church in more than a local and specific manner. It is conceivable that some prophetic messages may be for a diocese or for the universal Church and that some may be of more than passing value. All of this is said with considerable caution for fear of giving prophecy a sensational tone or false value. It clearly does not have the enduring value, for example, which Scripture has as the revealed and permanently recorded Word which God has left for the Church for all time. Nor does it carry with it the authority which the teaching power of the Church contains, but it is a vehicle by which God can speak at a given time with immediacy and power. There is no reason that that Word must necessarily be confined to a given moment in time and space. In fact, it is quite con-

ceivable that God could raise up prophetic ministries sent to bishops and the pope to speak God's Word to them, in a sense after
the model of St. Catherine of Siena.

Prophecy can be judged according to its uses. In an assembly,
it should contribute to the upbuilding of the assembly in an orderly
fashion without dominating it. When given for an individual, such
as Agabus' prophecy to Paul (Acts 21:10), it should be for consolation, exhortation and upbuilding related to the life and work of the
Church. In no sense can it be for gain or other improper motives.
Prophecy for unbelievers is to be judged by its ability to confront
them with the saving message of Christ. It is not to be judged by
its sensational value but by its effectiveness in leading them to conversion. A person can recognize a prophetic inspiration in the form
of an intelligible inspiration which appears to originate from the
Spirit. It may be sensed by words or phrases flashing across the
mind or by a strong conviction or sense that one should speak. It
may be accompanied by a physical sensation or anointing as well.
Sometimes when the gift is received words come in bursts or short
phrases. By calmly cooperating with the inspiration, clear patterns
will soon emerge. The inspiration should be tested by a brief critical examination, asking questions such as: "Did I make this up?"
It is also important to ask if the content and tone of the inspiration
lend themselves to the situation if the message is for a group. Is it
an appropriate time in the gathering for this message? It should be
noted that what is called for here is the use of reason. In some
prayer meetings some people simply speak out whatever comes to
them without thinking. It is necessary to think about (1) the validity of the message; (2) its appropriateness for the meeting; and (3)
at what precise point to speak. Where this is done and there is
doubt, a brief prayer for light will often leave a quiet impression,
either positive or negative, which can usually be trusted. If, after
testing it, the inspiration remains, the message should probably be
given. Support from others is very important to those exercising
the gift of prophecy. Charity requires that others give honest feedback. In cases where the prophetic message is for an individual
rather than a group, great caution should be used in delivering it.
Perhaps other prudent Christians should first be consulted. Such
inspirations, while valid, can also be harmful in frightening or in-

timidating individuals. They need to be tested in the cold critical light of common sense.

Prophecies call for a response. For them to be effective, those who hear must understand what kind of response they call for and how best to respond. Prophecies can be inspirational. They may serve to call people to turn to God more completely in repentance or worship. In such cases, a person hearing the prophecy should examine himself and humbly turn to God as generously as possible. Prophecies may speak of God's great love and mercy, thereby seeking to arouse a movement of the heart toward God. If so, the prophetic words should be allowed to penetrate the heart and should be savored, as it were, in one's mind even by repeating them when appropriate. At times, prophecies may call an individual to some action. When they stimulate the desire to act, the action should be prayerfully considered with proper caution proportionate to the significance of the action. If it is God's will, one should act upon it in love for God. For example, a prophetic inspiration to make a telephone call should receive less testing than a prophetic inspiration to buy a house. Both could be valid. Each should be carefully tested. If the action called for is unusual, unsettling, or disturbing in some fashion, the prophecy should be very cautiously and carefully tested before it is acted upon. When a prophecy predicts the future, special care should be taken. Some prophecies are used by God to tell the future in such a way as to forewarn of a possible course of events. When such predictions are determined to be authentic, they should be met with prayer and fasting. Another type of prophecy foretells the future by indicating what God intends to do so that one may know that he is God. Such prophecies are to be meditated upon rather than acted upon. For example, God may state that he is going to raise up a great work. As this happens, it is possible to recall his promise and praise him for it. At the beginning of the charismatic renewal among Catholics, a prophecy predicted its growth from coast to coast in a way that seemed impossible to the hundred or so people involved. Yet such growth did occur beyond any conceivable expectation. The response proper to such a prophecy is to praise and worship God.

False prophecy, fortunately, is rare. It does not build up or glorify Christ although it may sound spiritual. The exercise of such prophecy should be carefully corrected before harm is done to an individual or group. In cases where an individual has serious emotional problems, the use of the gift of prophecy should be carefully restricted. A person should be gently approached by leaders of a group and perhaps requested not to prophesy for a given time.

The renewal of the gift of prophecy in the charismatic renewal is an important event. The gift should be highly valued in the assembly of Christians. It is a means by which the whole Christian people can turn to God more completely.

c. Healing

The gift of healing has been experienced in the charismatic renewal with frequence. Although this gift has been exercised and experienced throughout the history of the Church, the charismatic renewal offers a new insight into the role and operation of this gift. Because it attracts attention, often arouses great expectations, and is not commonly understood or appreciated, the entire subject of healing will be treated here in a fuller manner than is required to treat the charismatic gift of healing itself.

1. God's Work Is a Work of Healing

Modern man is unlikely to believe that Christianity has anything significant to say about the area of sickness and healing. Today men are raised in an intellectual universe which cultivates an exclusive faith in empirical scientific method. According to this viewpoint, only those truths which can be arrived at by empirical method are true. It tends to associate any approach to sickness not firmly rooted in what is already known by modern medicine with primitive and superstitious attitudes toward illness. There are, however, limitations to scientific method. Especially in regard to the ultimate questions of life and death, scientific method is not able to shed much light. No one is in a better position to testify with humility to the limitations of medical knowledge than the practitioner of medicine himself.

Christianity, on the other hand, is competent to reflect upon these broader questions because the source of its understanding of reality does not come from human reason but is revealed from

God. Due to revelation, the Christian has an important insight into sickness and health which medicine can substantiate at points but cannot establish on its own authority.

Revelation offers an important insight into the nature of sickness. Illness had no place in God's original conception of life. It sprang from that disorder which jolted creation out of God's plan. Through disobedience, sin entered the world, and, through sin, death and sickness (cf. Rom. 5:12). Although Scripture is not scientific, its account of creation reveals an essential truth about sickness. It shows that sickness is a disorder which has entered creation. It links sickness to death and sin. Sickness, therefore, is an evil which represents a disruption of the natural order and it is not intended by God. God's attitude toward sickness thus should be clear. Sickness is an evil which God is working to remove. In this sense, God's work can be understood to be one of healing. He has worked to restore the natural order by supplanting it with another order, that of grace, in which the old creation is enveloped in a new and more wondrous creation. Sickness is one of the forces which will be absent from this new order. And even in the present creation as it awaits the completion of its redemption, God works to heal.

Even in the desert, God told Israel: "I am the Lord, your healer" (Ex. 15:26). His revelation in Christ reveals more completely his healing will. Jesus healed frequently and manifestly and conferred this power upon his disciples from their first mission (Mt. 10:1). The discourse at the conclusion of Mark's Gospel indicates the Church's understanding of healing as a sign accompanying believers. In Acts, the healing ministry is continued in the miraculous cures worked by the disciples (cf. Acts 3:1ff; 8:7; 9:32ff; 14:8ff; 28:8f). Healing occurred through a variety of methods: the laying on of hands, anointing with oil (Mk. 6:13; Jas. 5:14ff), touch, through Peter's shadow falling upon the sick (Acts 5:15), and through handkerchiefs touched by Paul (Acts 19:12). The ministry of healing and the gift of healing have continued to operate in the Church. They have marked the ministry of a number of the saints. Shrines such as Lourdes also testify to the presence of God's healing power in the Church today. The sacraments, too, are sources of healing (cf. 1 Cor. 11:29ff). Healing was a foretaste of the new life which Christ brought to man until the parousia when our bodies would be transformed. Healing served as a glimpse into that work of restoration. It was also, and more importantly, a sign of the deeper work which Christ accomplished. Healing symbolized the reconciliation of God and man through Christ. No longer did sin and death hold sway over man. Their power was broken through Christ's death and resurrection. Although this victory will not be complete until the end, healing is one way it breaks out in time.

2. Healing in a Christian Sense

Healing is a process which can be furthered in many ways. Because sickness runs counter to the natural order of things, there is much in the natural order that works to heal. In a vital way, the human body is an agent of healing. There is much merit in treatments which assist the body in its process of healing itself. The science of healing and its practitioners have applied reason and a disciplined approach to the area of healing and have been able to greatly further the process of healing. Some individuals possess certain natural gifts which aid the process of healing. Such individuals are able to promote healing through their presence and work and possess what might be described as a natural aptitude for healing. There are natural powers of healing inherent in body and mind which are barely understood and yet are real and effective. There are also spiritual forces which are able to effect the process of healing. In summary, there are many factors which relate to the process of healing.

We wish to consider healing here in a specifically Christian sense. Christian healing is the effect of Christ's redemption upon the process of healing of mind, soul, or body. Christian healing is not strictly of a miraculous nature as is sometimes supposed. It is a dimension of Christ's work of redemption which takes effect through the work of the Spirit in the lives of believers. Nor is Christian healing simply physical. It affects body, mind, and soul. Christ came to heal man's disordered relationship with God which is the ultimate cause of sickness. By forgiving sin, he furthers the work of healing of both body and mind. The charismatic renewal has prompted an awakening interest in the importance of seeking to apply Christ's healing power to those dimensions of life in which men are depressed, anxious, crippled by injuries, and pained by experiences from the past. Christ's power does heal inwardly and such healing can and should be sought. Christ also heals physical ailments. A particular work of healing often involves two or three of these areas in differing degrees.

Christian healing is a work of the Spirit which is very broad. It takes place at many levels of life through many means. In a universal sense, the Church is the principle agent of healing in the world. It is, in a sense, the sacrament of healing. The sacraments, Scripture, and the various vocations of Christians are channels of healing. The sacraments of penance and the anointing of the sick are specifically sacraments of healing. Through them, Christ ministers his healing power to men, touching them in soul and body. The Eucharist is also a source of healing. St. Paul, for example, chides the Corinthians for an inadequate appreciation of the body and blood of Christ and attributes some of their illnesses to their attitude (1 Cor. 11:30). Scripture and the proclamation of the Gospel are also means of healing.

God uses many different people in his work of healing. Christ heals, of course, through the vocations of those Christians who are especially associated with the care of mental or physical disorders. Through their dedication to duty and the practice of their skills, the Lord is able to bring comfort, consolation, and healing to many. Healing is a work which Christ seeks to perform through every Christian, as well. Each Christian encounters many situations in a lifetime where there is sickness or disorder. An individual can be an agent of Christ's healing power through living a devout life, through specific prayer for a situation, disorder, or illness, and, where appropriate, through action. Christ also works through a miraculous gift of healing which we will treat presently. It is our concern here to emphasize that healing is not simply a matter of miracles. Christ's grace is at work in many ways to heal physical, spiritual, and mental disorders. Insofar as it is ordered to eternal life, Christ's work of healing is always effective. Insofar as healing is ordered to this life, it is effective, although its effect is not always extraordinary or apparent. In this life, his work of healing is limited by the fact that all men will die.

3. *The Charismatic Gift of Healing*

At this point, we will take up the charismatic gift of healing. The gift of healing is a special gift of the Spirit. It is a gratuitous work of God by which the healing of body, mind or soul is substantially aided through the miraculous operation of the Holy Spirit. Although God's grace always works to heal, it does not always work in a miraculous way. A miraculous healing is marked by a substantial change in the condition of the patient due to the workings of the Spirit. These effects manifest themselves promptly if not instantly and result in a substantial improvement if not a complete healing. God heals in a miraculous way through a variety of agents, including the sacraments, the ministry of a priest, prayer, or the ministry of a healer. Healing can occur through the prayer of any Christian. The Spirit does, however, give the gift of healing to some individuals in a powerful way. These individuals are consistently agents over a period of time for miraculous healings.

The gift of healing has a tremendous value for the Church. It stands visibly as a sign of the power of Christ in a secular world. It awakens Christians to the reality of the deeper healing which Christ accomplishes and serves as a sign of the resurrection. Its exercise was important in the ministry of Jesus and the life of the early Church; its exercise in the fullest manner is important for the Church in the present time.

The positive value of this gift must be affirmed especially in light of its limitations. These limitations exist and need to be mentioned. As with all the charismatic gifts, the gift of healing is vulnerable to sensational exploitation. It is not always possible to determine with certainty that the gift has been operative. There are many aspects of illness and healing about which medical science knows little if anything. And so, some healings labeled as miraculous may simply be due to the operation of natural forces. Healing is an area in which exploitation of the gullible is especially possible, and there is a long and sorry record of Christian healers whose ministry was attended by misunderstanding, heartache, and confusion. Those who are in need of healing in their anguish are unlikely to consider credentials or exercise prudence in seeking comfort. Ministries which inflate hopes or emphasize emotional excesses do no good to God and bring no merit. Healers operating in such a style should be encouraged to change. Fakes should be diligently exposed.

Those who have received the charismatic gift of healing deserve special support and love. The gift itself does not imply either sanctity or wisdom. Nor is it necessarily accompanied by an understanding of the nature of the gift. Christians with healing ministries need encouragement in the exercise of their ministry. They also need friends who will help keep their pride from swelling. A healer is part of the body—no superman—and needs the ministry and support of other ministries in the body. It is especially important that those with healing ministries attend diligently to their own spiritual growth.

The operation of the gift of healing has inspired a variation of a doctrine of faith which can be dangerous and absurd. The underlying theory, which has merit, is God's desire to heal and the importance of expectant faith on the part of the individual. In regard to the gift of healing, it has been maintained that healing can be obtained without exception through an act of faith. Of course, it follows that if there is no healing the cause was inadequate faith. This doctrine produces sad but comical results, such as people seeking to work themselves up emotionally to an act of faith or "claiming a healing in faith" over a long period of an illness which obviously has not been healed in any extraordinary way. Regrettably, it also produces feelings of guilt, fear, or inferiority.

4. Some Conclusions Regarding Christian Healing

a. *A Proper Attitude toward Healing.* In the charismatic renewal, God is reviving a general appreciation of his work of healing. He is calling individual Christians and the entire Church to understand the importance of healing. Christians should cultivate a positive attitude toward healing. Throughout their lives they will find themselves in numerous situations where they can be agents of God's healing power. The principle which should guide them is that it is God's will to heal and restore. As a result, Christians should work in every way wherever possible to further healing. In addition to using whatever skills are available, prayer is a very important factor in healing. In dealing with sickness, one should boldly pray for healing unless there is a very good reason not to do so. Prayer for healing should be a normal part of the remedy for illness.

b. *Seeking Healings.* Charismatic healing should also be sought. A person should pray in faith, earnestly seeking the miraculous operation of God's Spirit. If one is simple and sincere, God's response will be understood. It is certain that God always works for the best. In seeking a miraculous healing, we may wish to request the prayers and ministry of someone with a recognized gift of healing. As long as this quest is prompted by a love of God and a basic resignation to his will, such attempts will be pleasing to him. The prayers of someone with such a gift can be very important.

When we pray for healing, it should be with full expectation and often. Faith is an important factor in miraculous healings. It is something which Christ required of many of those whom he healed, and great displays of faith often moved him to heal. It must frankly be recognized that God is often rebuffed in his desire to heal by a lack of openness to miraculous healing. One should seek to cultivate an expectant faith in God's healing power.

On the other hand, as was mentioned above, there is a danger in over-emphasizing the role of faith. Some charismatics, believing that God always works to heal miraculously, insist that faith is the only ingredient absent. As a result, they would maintain that where there is sufficient faith, miraculous healing always occurs. Such a position is unacceptable. Despite the presence of great faith, God does not always heal miraculously. For example, St. Paul was a man of great faith and one whom God used to heal others miraculously. Yet he himself was sick (Gal. 4:13), he left one of his helpers, Trophimus, ill at Miletus (2 Tm. 4:19), and he advised his disciple Timothy to take a little wine for the sake of his stomach and his frequent ailments (1 Tm. 5:23). Furthermore, one of his companions was Luke, "the beloved physician" (1 Cor. 14:14). If God always worked to heal in a miraculous way, Paul would have surely been able to cure himself, to cure Trophimus instead of leaving him behind, and to cure Timothy or suggest that someone heal him instead of suggesting a natural remedy. In addition, Luke would have been out of work and would have been the "well-beloved ex-physician." As it is, though, miraculous healings are not available to every Christian upon demand by faith. They are a gift which God gives freely according to his will. To seek to stir up one's faith by a superhuman act and thus facilitate a healing can be offensive. Also an extreme emphasis upon the role of faith can cause guilt or depression on the part of someone not experiencing a miraculous cure.

In praying for a miraculous healing for another person, we should be guided by prudence and charity. If moved to pray with someone in an extraordinary way, we should proceed with great caution. If prayer for healing would upset the person, for example, quiet prayer in his presence without disturbing him might be better. We should not arouse false expectations, but rather lead a person to greater dependence upon Christ.

Despite the fact that there are times when he does not heal miraculously, God's work is always a healing work. No earnest prayer goes unheeded. Even when there is no physical healing, he works to perform healings of spirit and mind. It must be said, though, that he probably would work more miraculous healings were he given the opportunity.

c. *Prayers Are Answered.* Whether a miraculous healing is sought or not, it is important to respect the power of God to heal and pray for healing in the face of all sickness or distress. God always answers such prayers. In cases where their effects are not visible, it may be necessary to wait, perhaps until the end of time, to understand what has happened and why. Their effect, united in Christ's glorious work of salvation, will be manifest in the glorious body of the saints gathered in the praise of God.

d. *Respect for Natural Means of Healing.* In praying for

healing, the role of nature and science must be recognized. It is important to take proper care and precautions and to seek medical assistance where necessary.

e. *Inner Healing.* Prayer for inner healing—or, as it is known, the "healing of memories"—can sometimes be helpful in growing in the Christian life. In the course of such a prayer, past incidents are recalled and God's healing power is explicitly sought. It is important that any personal sin be recognized and, where necessary, confessed, and that any resentments be dropped and forgiveness extended to all. A mature Christian can be of help in such a prayer. It can be fruitfully linked with penance and reception of the Eucharist. From time to time, the process of seeking inner healing will be of value in dealing with hurts or disappointments. This prayer has a twofold advantage of helping us to turn to God for help with major interior problems and of teaching us to do so in an ongoing way.

f. *Sickness and Personal Sin.* It is wrong to equate sickness with personal sin. Neither the blind man nor his parents in the Gospel story sinned, yet he was blind (Jn. 9:2). Sickness was not, strictly speaking, retribution for sin but an evil resulting from the sinful separation of man from God.

g. *Claims for Healing.* Claims can rashly be made for miraculous healings. It is important to respect the distinction between a miracle and a regular work of healing in which God's grace was operative. Both are healings and both give God glory. It is possible, though, to speak of a normal process of healing in such a way as to discredit ourselves, Christianity, the charismatic renewal, and the miraculous gift of healing. For example, by claiming without qualification a "healing" of an ailment that gradually goes away, it is possible to stir up skepticism. Caution is especially needed in speaking of healing to non-Christians. It is important to avoid the loose use of terms such as "I was healed" and to avoid excessive, unqualified, or unfounded claims. There is much merit in letting time pass and in seeking medical advice before speaking of a miraculous occurrence. One must take care not to shade the truth in favor of the extraordinary out of any misguided desire to give the Lord extra exposure.

h. *Normal Medical Procedures.* Under no circumstances should anyone be encouraged or encourage anyone to stop normal medical procedures or consultation as a result of a suspected or anticipated healing. In such cases a person may be told, for example, that he is healed of heart trouble and should stop taking medicine. If such advice is given to another person, we should in good will strongly take exception to it. If God has healed, a physician will be able to tell. To act rashly or lightly advise someone in this matter would be the height of folly. Even our Lord obeyed religious and civic law as well as custom in regard to his healings—for example, by sending the lepers who were healed to the priests so that they might be inspected and officially pronounced "cured" (cf. Mt. 8:4).

i. *The Role of Suffering.* As a result of the awareness among charismatics of God's multiple works of healing, there is a need for them to re-evaluate their understanding of suffering. A renewal of Catholic spirituality in regard to the role of suffering is in process in our time, and the charismatic renewal, in this respect, is in harmony with a general movement of the Spirit in the Church. It must be admitted that much of the popular spiritual teaching in past years regarding healing and sickness has been deficient. There has been too much of an imbalance in favor of humbly accepting suffering as a source of grace. In its extreme, this spirituality was more stoic than Christian, and at its worst it was morbid and unhealthy. Happily, the charismatic renewal emphasizes elements such as the healing power of God which brings another, more positive perspective.

There is, however, a danger in the renewal—as there has been in the post-conciliar Church as a whole—of popular teaching going to the opposite extreme. In such a candy-colored spirituality, there is for the Christian only happiness, joy, and goodness in this life. Such notions are naive. It is necessary to remember in an authentic spirituality that death still separates an individual from the full experience of the resurrection and that death is an ugly prospect even for a Christian. There is, furthermore, suffering and sickness to be endured in the course of this life. Suffering is an evil. It is an evil, though, which has meaning for a Christian. Through suffering, one shares in Christ's suffering. "We bear in our body the sufferings of the death of Jesus, so that the life of Jesus also may be seen in our body" (2 Cor. 4:10). The death of Jesus was a brutal and ugly affair which he endured and despised—so the author of Hebrews says—"for the joy that was set before him" (Heb. 12:2). Suffering, sickness, and death are repulsive. God's grace ordinarily does not soften their effect. It strengthens one inwardly by consoling, supporting, and enabling one to compare present sufferings "with the glory that is to be revealed" (Rom. 8:18). There are special gifts by which suffering can easily be endured. These gifts cannot be presumed. There is, however, a deep joy available to all who love Jesus in sharing in his sufferings. It is possible in suffering to be united with Jesus crucified in a special and powerful manner. There are times when our only prayer can be to place ourselves at the foot of the cross. The love of Christ and his people has caused some to welcome suffering as a means of completing "what is lacking in Christ's afflictions for the sake of his body, that is, the Church" (Col. 1:24). We must look upon such love as a deep mystery which God in his own time will reveal. It is sufficient here to note that suffering has a place in the Christian life and that sickness is one way of suffering. Yet sickness, when God does not work to heal, is still an evil which must be endured and despised.

j. *Every Christian a Healer.* A person should seek to understand how God wishes to use him to heal, and should pray for healings whenever appropriate. It is especially valuable to cultivate the habit of praying for healing in Christian homes and with children. Such prayers should be accompanied by seeking normal remedies. Using remedies does not render prayer useless or void of faith. Visitation of the sick in hospitals or homes is important, too. On the last day Christ will say to some Christians: "I was sick . . . and you did not visit me" (Mt. 25:43). Sickness is a time when we are especially subject to depression or discouragement. Through love, sensitivity, consideration, and prayers, we should seek to bring encouragement and hope to the sick. In so doing, it is Jesus himself who is served.

The revival in the charismatic renewal of an appreciation of healing and the manifestation of the gift of healing are happy events for the Church. Through the mystery of this gift, it is possible to glimpse Christ himself, the great physician. It is important to understand healing, pray for it, and pray for those who are healers whether through natural means or by the extraordinary gift of healing.

7. Some Conclusions about the Gifts

In conclusion, the value of the charismatic gifts must be recognized. These gifts can be exercised by any Christian but are commonly experienced in the charismatic renewal because their importance is appreciated and their exercise cultivated. Persons who have received the charismatic experience should welcome the exercise of charismatic gifts. When used with ordinary common sense, they can contribute to God's glory. They should not be regarded as a source of fear or apprehension but as tools which can build the body of Christ if used properly. It is more important that their proper use be encouraged in a positive manner than that grim warnings be issued regarding possible excesses. By encouraging a balanced understanding of the gifts, any improper emphasis will be avoided. Above all, it is necessary for charismatics to remember those who will stand before the Lord at the last day, claiming to have worked mighty deeds, prophesied, and cast out demons whom he will disown (Mt. 7:22-23). We should cultivate the gifts seriously and cultivate love more seriously (cf. 1 Cor. 14:1). By training our hearts to turn to God in love in the exercise of the gifts, they can glorify God and work for our salvation.

VI
Charismatic Community

A. Church and Community

Especially among Catholics, the charismatic movement has been accompanied by a widespread interest in community. Although this interest has taken different forms, it marks almost every expression of the charismatic renewal. Interest in community is a natural and healthy consequence of such a movement. Its roots are threefold:

1. The dynamic of sharing a powerful experience draws people together into closer association. The mechanisms of the charismatic renewal, such as prayer meetings and teaching, promote and reinforce this natural desire for community.

2. There is a general need for community in modern society. Today, almost every institution which once met legitimate needs for friendship and support is disintegrating. The communities of the past, such as the local civic community, the neighborhood, and the parish or church community, have almost ceased to exist for most Americans as a meaningful source of friendship or association. The family which is the sole surviving institution is under heavy attack both because of the frequency and availability of divorce and the conditions which promote it and because of the distances which commonly separate members of the larger family circle. As a result of this disintegration, many people experience a community-vacuum. The charismatic group fills that vacuum.

3. On a deeper level, there is inherent in any action of the Holy Spirit an inspiration toward community. The formation of communities is an impulse which marks an authentic spiritual awakening. By the Spirit's action, there emerges in an individual an aptitude for community and an intuitive appreciation of its role

in the Christian life. Furthermore, in history the pattern of God's action has been shaped by his plan to form a people.

In the charismatic renewal, these factors combine to make the desire for community an omnipresent force apparent to even its most casual observers. Such a desire strikes very deep cords in man and awakens powerful inner forces. The desire for community requires careful examination as one of the most significant implications of the charismatic experience.

The immediate communitarian reality which affects most charismatics is the local charismatic group or community. It is usually in the midst of this group that an individual is drawn into the charismatic experience, and the group is, so to speak, the womb of an individual's explicit or deepened Christianity. The group rapidly becomes the focal point for primary relationships. As such, it is a powerful force in a charismatic's life. The fact that the initial experience of community is in a charismatic community can easily lead to an improper identification of Christian community with charismatic community. Therefore, it is necessary at the outset of any consideration of the role of community in the charismatic renewal to set the ideal of community in its proper perspective.

1. The Church as Community

In the first place, charismatic community, like the charismatic renewal itself, can only be adequately understood in reference to the Church. The Church is the Christian community par excellence; it is the font from which every instance of community flows. The Church is the community of faith established by Christ and gathered around the successors of Peter and the apostles. It is a visible society on earth with a hierarchial structure. It is the visible manifestation of the Kingdom of God in which the divine and human are interlocked into one whole. Specific Christian communities may come and go, but the Christian community or Church will remain.

It is possible for charismatics to underestimate the importance of the Church. There is considerable misunderstanding abroad regarding institution and authority. This prejudice, particularly virulent in the twentieth century, coupled with extreme individualistic forms of piety, makes it possible for many to read modern notions into the scriptural writings. The popular conclusion is that no authority or structure could be consistent with the teachings of Jesus. This deep-seated notion is reinforced in some instances by the experience of charismatics. The groups through which they have received the charismatic experience contrast favorably with their general experience of Christianity. The fervor of the groups bespeaks a sincerity and itself generates enthusiasm. It must be sadly admitted that such critical comparisons often have serious grounds. The Church has not been able to communicate the evangelical fervor to many of its members. A well-articulated and forceful pentecostal teaching reinforces these impressions. Its thesis is: "Come out of the established Churches and form the true Church." Variously interpreted, this doctrine, known as "come-out-ism" in some circles, grew as a result of early pentecostal experience with and suspicion of established Churches. Its effects have been pernicious among main-line Protestant denominations but only peripheral among Catholics. Nevertheless, the combination of these forces can serve to dull and blunt the Spirit's work of inspiring a deep love for the Church.

As a result, it is necessary here to attempt to formulate some thoughts which may aid in understanding the Church. Although by no means the basis of a systematic treatise, they do provide a basic framework by which Catholic charismatics can evaluate their understanding of the Church; hopefully they will also be of assistance to other charismatic Christians as well.

1. Jesus established the Church. The Church is not an accident, a coincidence, or the work of disciples such as Paul. The Scriptures make it apparent that Jesus intended to establish an ongoing community which would continue in his stead. His actions demonstrate a clear purpose and direction. He deliberately gathered a group of disciples and formed them into a community based on faith in him. He taught them, revealed the mysteries of the Kingdom to them (Mt. 13:10-17), and prepared them for their mission. They baptized (Jn. 4:2), preached, cast out spirits, and healed the sick (Mk. 6:7-13). He taught them about the importance of

service and humility as opposed to pride and honor in their inter-relationships (Mk. 9:35). He taught them to seek out lost souls (Mt. 10:6), the value of common prayer (Mt. 18:19-20), and the importance of seeking to reconcile sinners before expelling them (Mt. 18:15-18). He predicted his death to them and referred to their continued existence in the discourses on the persecution they were to face (Mt. 10:17-25; Jn. 15:18—16:4), and on the make-up of the Christian community as a group of sinners and just (Mt. 22:11ff; 13:24-43, 47-50). In Matthew 16:18, he compares the Church to a building founded on a rock which will endure even the attacks of Satan. Although the word "Church" appears only twice in the Gospels (Mt. 16:18; 18:17), the idea of an on-going community which will attract disciples and continue his work is clearly that of Jesus. The actions of the early Christians reflect their conviction that Christ established them as a community. They quickly filled the place left vacant by Judas (Acts 2:22). They gathered together regularly, established new offices to meet needs, and, in short, continued as the living community which Jesus founded.

At first, many are taken aback at the thought of attributing a deliberate methodology to Jesus. However, it must be apparent to even the most casual reader of the Gospels that Jesus was a man seriously intent upon God's business. Reflection upon his work will reveal its effects. In a few years, he executed a plan which was to have massive repercussions on life and history. Although he worked in a way that might seem unlikely in one intent upon establishing a Kingdom, there is a deliberate purpose evident in his work. The wisdom and simplicity of his method almost hides this intent. He formed his followers into an enduring community of faith which was sealed by the Holy Spirit at Pentecost. It matters little whether the details and specifics were set down by him or whether there was a written constitution. Like any wise leader, he concentrated his efforts on forming a community, endowing it with his principles, and communicating his spirit. Unlike any other leader, he was divine, and consequently the community of faith which he established was unlike any other human institution, sharing in its essence his divine character.

2. Jesus instituted sacraments in the Church as privileged

channels of grace. He deliberately left the Church signs and vehicles by which his presence could be experienced in a profound way. The Eucharist is the principal sacrament. In a deliberate act recorded in the Gospels and referred to by Paul, Jesus blessed bread and wine and distributed it as his body and blood, commanding that this action be done in memory of him. St. John records Jesus as teaching that unless a man eats his body and drinks his blood, he cannot have life. When it became a point of difficulty for some, he let them fall away rather than retreat from his statement (Jn. 6:60). Christ's deliberate and conscious act in the context of the celebration of the Passover—Israel's deliverance from Egypt—which recalled the inauguration of the first covenant makes it apparent that Jesus was consciously establishing a new covenant and that the Eucharist was to be the sign of that covenant. The other sacraments have a basis in Scripture and Christian practice. It is clear that baptism and the rite conferring the Spirit with the laying on of hands were part of the experience of the early Christians. Christ conferred the power to forgive sins. Likewise, offices in the Church were conferred with special prayers, the sick were anointed, and marriage, signifying the love of Christ for the Church (Eph. 5:32), required its special gift (1 Cor. 7:7).

The New Testament does not, of course, contain a sacramental theology, nor does Jesus give a treatise on the sacraments. However, it is clear that he instituted rites for which the early Church claimed an efficacy never asserted for Jewish ritual and which were regarded as integral to Christ's work of salvation. Gradually the Church has come to understand the nature of the sacraments and to distinguish them from other Christian actions and prayers as being a permanent sign of grace, instituted by Christ, and efficacious *ex opere operato*. Through the sacraments, Christ acts in an immediate and special way to sanctify his people.

3. The essentials of structure and authority were established by Christ and already existed in the early Church. Jesus appointed leaders for the primitive community (cf. Mt. 28:18-20; 18:18; Jn. 20:21-23; 21:15-17). The Gospels relate his selection of twelve apostles and the special training which they received. John especially reveals the special teaching given to these apostles on the na-

ture of leadership in the Christian Kingdom. As leaders they were to differ from the world's leaders, and Christ took pains to emphasize the difference. There was continuity of leadership among the disciples after the ascension. Acts records as their first concern the replacement of Judas. It was the recognized leadership of the community, furthermore, which proposed the creation of a new office, that of deacon, to assist in ministry to the Church. Acts and the Epistles testify to the existence of authority and structure in the various churches. Paul appointed elders in the churches he established (Acts 14:23), and various officers of the community are mentioned throughout the New Testament (1 Thes. 5:12-13; Phil. 1:1; 1 Pt. 5:1-5; Heb. 13:24; Ti. 1:5-9; 1 Tm. 3). Although the nature of these various offices may not have been precisely defined, it is clear from the New Testament that they exercised extensive authority within the Christian community. Paul's letters, for example, reveal a primitive but consistent and formulated view of his perogatives as apostle. The non-canonical writings of the early Church, such as the *Epistle of Clement* and the epistles of Ignatius of Antioch, also testify to the presence within the Church of a firmly established structure. Ignatius, bishop of Antioch, wrote seven letters before his martyrdom during the reign of Trajan. These letters date before 117 A.D. or less than seventy-five years after the death of Christ. In one, he writes: "Avoid divisions; they are the beginning of evil. All of you should obey the bishop—as Jesus obeyed the Father—and the body of elders as you would the apostles. And revere the deacons as God's will. No one should do any of the things pertaining to the Church without the bishop. That is to be considered an authentic eucharistic liturgy which is celebrated by the bishop or his legitimate substitute. The congregation should be present wherever the bishop appears, just as the Catholic Church is wherever Jesus Christ is. It is not allowed to baptize or to conduct an agape without the bishop. But whatever he approves is also pleasing to God. In this way, everything you do will be true and valid."

In this letter, as well as in the other letters, Ignatius provides a picture of the Christian community in which the bishop exercises a key function. Nor were the churches isolated and independent units. The church in Jerusalem took it upon itself to send Peter and John to visit the newly converted disciples in Samaria and to minister to them (Acts 8:14-25) and to send Barnabas to the church in Antioch. The leaders of the entire Church gathered to decide the thorny question of the Gentiles and the law. Their decision was related to the congregation at Antioch as if it were binding there. Furthermore, Paul himself, who takes pains to demonstrate that his apostleship is from God, also takes pains to submit his ministry to the discernment of the apostles (Gal. 2:1-10). Paul did not hesitate to exercise his authority over the churches he founded or ministered to, and he even addressed the Roman church with authority although a stranger. This inter-relationship among the churches deepened and continued. Clement, for example, as bishop of Rome took it upon himself to address a letter of admonition to the Corinthians.[1] An examination of the early Church leaves the distinct impression of structure and authority within local assemblies and a unity among all the churches which was considered by the first Christians as consistent with Jesus' teaching and established by him in its essential features.

It is possible, of course, to compare the Church today with the early Church and concentrate upon the differences. It may help to reflect upon the analogy which the institution of the American presidency presents. When the American Constitution was drafted, the office of president was not envisioned as it exists today. The framers of the Constitution would be shocked at the enormous reservoir of power at the disposal of the president today. It is a far cry from the times of Washington, yet few would argue that the institution is not the same. It has evolved and grown as the nation has grown and expanded. In its essence, though, it is the same institution. In considering the Church, it also helps to reflect upon the changes wrought by growth and expansion. Now numbering more than half a billion members, it has different needs than the early Church. Twenty centuries have also made a profound difference in the Church and its offices. However, the difference in appearance from the early Church does not mean that the institution is not basically the same.

Furthermore, in considering the Church, there is a great danger in thinking primarily in terms of political or juridical models, as with the constitutional analogy used here. Jesus' work in establishing the Church was not primarily political or constitutional. Although the Church is an institution, and founded as such by Christ, it is a mistake to view it primarily in an institutional framework. The essence of the Church's nature is that it is the continuation of Christ's presence in the world. In establishing the new Israel, Jesus' concern was not so much to form a codified law like that of Moses, or a ritual like that of the temple, but to establish a people of faith out of the people of Israel. His teaching could be compared to a seed containing within itself all the elements which were to manifest themselves. Jesus constituted the Church by assembling his disciples and conferring the gift of his Spirit. Over the centuries the implications of Christ's teaching became clearer as the Church reflected upon revelation and studied Scripture and the traditions handed down from the apostles in light of new challenges, questions, and opportunities as they arose. Aided by the Holy Spirit, the Church's understanding of Christ's teaching about its essential nature grew according to the demands of time and situation. In regard to structure and authority it remained faithful to the commission of Christ who had established a unified community of disciples, appointed leaders for the community, and commissioned Peter to feed the flock.

The process by which the Church gradually grew to understand its nature did not occur only in regard to structure and authority. Truths revealed by Christ such as the Trinity and his own divinity also evolved over time in the understanding of the Church. Nonetheless, with regard to structure and authority, the essential aspects of the unity of the entire Church, the existence of authority, its relationship to the authority of the apostles, and the primacy accorded to Peter are all apparent from the outset. As the Church grew, its understanding of its nature as an institution and the significance of its offices has grown. Vatican II, for example, continued this process by defining the role of the bishop with a clarity heretofore lacking, although it only stated truths that have been exercised in practice since the earliest days of the Church. The structure and authority of the Church have evolved and grown over twenty centuries. Its growth, guided by the Holy Spirit, rests upon essential elements of structure and authority established by Christ himself and apparent in the early Christian community.

4. The Church was established as a visible society in this world. The nature of its unity was not just a nebulous spiritual bond but a unity which came from membership in the community which Jesus established and through participation in the Eucharist. The fact that it was a real society and institution in this world did not make it an ordinary human institution. Because it was established by Christ and possessed his Spirit, it was in some measure a participation in the Kingdom of heaven. Like the field sown with wheat and tares, the Church is to remain until the end a perplexing mixture of human and divine (cf. Mt. 13:24-30).

5. The Church is the normal vehicle which God uses for salvation. God intended to save the world by calling a people to himself. He chose Israel, and the Church is the legitimate successor of his chosen people. It is the means through which God intends to establish his Kingdom, and it is through membership in the Church that a person belongs to Christ. Insisting on membership in the Church as the normal means of salvation is not to say that God does not or cannot work outside it. There are many men of good will and many devout Christians outside the Church. There are also ecclesial communities which play an important role in the work of salvation. These exceptional works of grace, however, do not alter God's ultimate intention, which is for men to be saved through one visible body in communion with one another.

6. The Church will be revealed in the fullness of its splendor at the end of time. She will be the bride of Christ, pure and glorious. The Church in this world, however, is not hidden or invisible. The Church, "constituted and organized in the world as a society, subsists in the Catholic Church, which is governed by the successor of Peter and by the bishops in union with that successor, although many elements of sanctification and of truth can be found outside of its visible structure" (*Constitution on the Church*, n. 8). This truth can be known by faith. Its validity stems from Christ who is the head of the Church. It is necessary and important that all to whom this knowledge of the Church is apparent must be loyal to it. The Church, as such, is an object of faith, love and obedience. It stands not simply or primarily as an institution

or human society, although these aspects are integral to its nature on earth, but as mother of the faithful and the bride of Christ. It is the duty of its sons and daughters to cultivate a filial love for it. Furthermore, obedience is owed to the Church and its shepherds, for they speak in the name of Christ by the power of the Holy Spirit.

By inspiring charismatics with a love of community, the Spirit is, above all, drawing them to a deeper union with their ecclesial community. The impulse toward community which the Holy Spirit has given to Catholics in the charismatic renewal is an impulse for communion with the Catholic Church.

This impulse toward fuller love of the Church is a precious and wondrous gift which must be treasured and cultivated. It is important that local groupings or charismatic communities in no way obstruct or usurp this impulse of love for the Church. Because of their powerful influence on charismatics, it would be possible for them to claim for themselves the fullness of devotion and loyalty due to the Church and its shepherds or, by failing to actively promote a love of the Church, become the object of such devotion by omission. Many of these communities are discovering experientially principles of authority and order which are essential for the life of the Church. These principles should apply even more to the universal Church. It is important for charismatics and charismatic communities to encourage in every way love and obedience for the Church, thereby rooting this impulse toward community in Christ's full plan for his people and insuring its proper development for individuals and charismatic communities alike.

Love of the Church can be cultivated in a variety of ways. Among Catholics, regular participation in the Eucharist is a valuable means of joining with the entire Church in worship. It is also important to become acquainted with the teachings of the Church. Every Catholic charismatic should own and study a copy of the documents of the Second Vatican Council. The letters of local bishops are also an important means of pastoral teaching, as are the letters and addresses of the Holy Father. The weekly English-language edition of *L'Osservatore Romano* is a wellspring of inspiration. It features the Holy Father's weekly teaching at his general audiences and is a powerful means by which the Spirit can speak. It is also important that individual charismatics and groups keep in close touch with pastors and bishops, seeking pastoral guidance and direction. Whenever possible or prudent, participation in the activities of local parishes can be a concrete means of participating in the Church.

2. The Ecumenical Dimension of the Charismatic Renewal

One of the most welcome characteristics of the charismatic renewal is its ecumenical dimension. It is a timely and important aspect of this movement, for it brings together elements of Christianity historically quite alien to each other. Already the charismatic movement has contributed to the unity of Christians in various ways and on various levels. The unity of all Christians is a matter of profound concern for every Christian. The wounds in the body of Christ from divisions among Christians are a source of sorrow and scandal. It is the duty of every Christian to work for unity in whatever way possible.

Ecumenism is an especially important issue in the charismatic renewal. With few exceptions, anyone receiving the charismatic experience is placed in an ecumenical environment. Any attempt to consider the charismatic Christian community must address its ecumenical dimensions. An attempt at a balanced approach toward ecumenism is difficult. Such an attempt must emphasize and encourage the positive growth of the spirit of Christian unity while cautioning against distortions of authentic ecumenism. This is an issue which is emotionally charged and one in which there is considerable confusion. What we attempt to do here is to offer some reflections on this area based on the *Decree on Ecumenism* of the Second Vatican Council. While this decree is a most appropriate guide for Catholics, it also formulates principles of considerable benefit to all Christians.

(a) Some Principles Drawn from the Decree on Ecumenism

1. It is Christ's deep desire "that all may be one" (Jn. 7:23). This desire is manifest in our times in the various movements for

unity among Christians. The unity of the Church has been a matter of concern from its very beginnings and is today a matter of great concern.

2. The disagreements which led to the separations of the Catholic Church with the Orthodox Churches and those of the Reformation were developments for which both sides were partially to blame.

3. The Catholic Church recognizes not only the Christian faith and brotherhood existing between individual Christians but also recognizes the corporate nature of the communities and Churches which are separated. Significant elements and endowments for the life of the Church can and do exist outside of the Catholic Church, and these communities and churches can be and are sources of grace and salvation. They have significance and importance in the mystery of salvation.

4. The Catholic Church sees defects and inadequacies in doctrine, discipline, or structure according to the various differences. For example, some of these communities or churches lack a sacramental system. In the eyes of the Catholic Church, those not in full communion with it "are not blessed by that unity which Jesus Christ wished to bestow on all. . . . For it is through Christ's Catholic Church alone, which is the all-embracing means of salvation, that the fullness of the means of salvation can be obtained. It was to the apostolic college alone, of which Peter is the head, that we believe that our Lord entrusted all the blessings of the new covenant, in order to establish on earth the one body of Christ into which all those should be fully incorporated who already belong in any way to God's people" (Decree on Ecumenism, n. 3).

(b) Some Reflections and Advice

1. Unity among Christians must be based upon mutual respect, loyalty to the truth, and love of Christ. The unity which Christ seeks to achieve in the Church is not a political unity; it is a unity of minds and hearts joined in his praise. It is important to avoid a false ecumenism which ignores or dismisses the differences between Christians as insignificant. They are not insignificant, and a pragmatic approach to unity can only lead to confusion.

2. It is necessary to renew one's own life in Christ as a preliminary step to ecumenical dialogue. Such renewal involves reaffirming one's faith in Christ according to the lights which God has given. For Catholics, this means coming to a living faith in the teachings of Christ as understood and taught in the Church. Any attempt at unity which is not founded in an understanding and appreciation of one's own tradition is shallow and limiting. Christians of every denomination should seek nourishment in the font of their own tradition and spirituality.

3. It is necessary to have a change of heart for there to be authentic ecumenism. New attitudes of love and yearning for unity must be cultivated as well as a deep-seated respect for other Christians and other Christian traditions.

4. In the charismatic renewal, unity can best be fostered by common worship at prayer meetings. Because of their spontaneous character these activities lend themselves especially to ecumenical prayer. It is in the common worship of Christ and the realization of the quickening power of the Spirit that charismatic Christians can come together. Furthermore, they can join together in common cause to bring an awareness of this work of the Spirit into the mainstreams of their various denominations. In a movement such as the charismatic which is ecumenical, tensions and areas of confusion inevitably arise. It is a mistake to gloss over ecumenical problems. They exist and must be faced.

The ecumenical problem most frequently faced by prayer groups and communities relates to the nature of the group. Usually in what is called the Catholic charismatic renewal at some point a decision must be made as to whether the major emphasis of the group will be Catholic or non-denominational. In such situations, merits and problems attach to either decision, and in every case the decision should be attended by reflection, discussion, prayer, and a sincere attempt to follow the leadings of the Spirit. Groups which decide to emphasize their Catholic nature are not necessarily unecumenical or closed to non-Catholics. A Catholic group can and should be ecumenical, in my opinion. Such groups which have grown from a Catholic background and in which a sizable majority of the members are Catholics have sought to respond to the graces of the Spirit by building a community and spirituality which actively affirms the Church. Attempts at non-denominational communities and groups also have advantages, although they pose serious questions touching upon the nature of the charismatic movement. Catholics involved in the charismatic renewal should welcome opportunities to grow in love with other Christians who are not Catholics. They must do so, however, seeking all the while to cultivate their own heritage of faith and seeking to grow in it. In this task they must avoid imprudent actions, respect the discipline of the Church, and especially seek the advice of pastors and bishops regarding these problems. Their attitude should certainly not be one of militantly trying to "convert" non-Catholics or disturb their faith; rather they should encourage each to be united to Christ in the fullest manner available by seeking to be united with the Church according to their understanding of it. By growing in love and respecting differences, Christ himself will be able to bridge them and establish the unity that all desire and pray for.

3. Communities within the Church

Although the Church is the Christian community in the fullest sense, communities within the Church have a significance in God's plan. The practice of associating together in community dates from the beginnings of the Church. The Christians at Jerusalem held all things in common and seem to have lived an intense communal life (cf. Acts 2:43-47; 4:32-37). Throughout the history of the Church, associations of Christians sharing their lives together in some fashion have existed. Some of these communities and associations have been formally recognized by the Church, such as the religious orders. Others of a more informal nature have existed in harmony with the Church. Through them, the community life of the Church is manifested and experienced in an immediate and vital manner. They are also an apostolic agent in the world, reaching many through the lives of their members who would not otherwise hear the Gospel. In addition, they provide their members with an opportunity to live out a more intense life of faith in association with others of like mind. They provide an environment which contributes to growth in brotherly love and holiness.

The rapid shift in institutional patterns marking modern life which makes the experience of community rare and precious increases the importance of such communities for the Church. It is opportune that when traditional patterns of community in Western society are collapsing the Church should be growing in an understanding of her social and communitarian dimension so as to be able to encourage community. They do offer, in some sense, a challenge to traditional patterns of organization of the pastoral ministry of the Church. However, where there is love and obedience to the bishops, any difficulties can be fruitfully resolved. They offer the Church a promising pastoral approach to modern society.

4. Charismatic Communities

Specific communities exist in the charismatic renewal. They have emerged at an astonishing rate and seem to be an inevitable outgrowth of the renewal. There is much to be said in favor of charismatic communities. They have contributed significantly to the stability of the charismatic movement. They offer an environment in which the implications of the charismatic experience can be lived out. They have, indeed, all the advantages which have been attributed to communities in general, with the added advantage that the charismatic experience provides an impetus and basis for serious community.

Charismatic communities also involve difficulties which must be faced. They tend to create a dynamic which could isolate them from the Church and the world. Not all isolation, of course, is bad, and some is necessary in order to concentrate upon a common goal. Nonetheless, the tendency to exclusiveness must be carefully checked.

The place of marriage and family within charismatic communities is a matter of considerable importance. In the eyes of Christ and the Church, "the family has received from God its mission to be the first and vital cell of society" (*Decree on the Apostolate of the Laity*, n. 11). Marriage must be held sacred, and charismatic communities must work to uphold and support marriage and the family. Any communitarian situation places stresses on the family. It must be the concern of couples and of charismatic communities to insure that such stresses result in positive growth in mutual love and affection between husband and wife and between parents and children. Community also raises the possibility of economic cooperation and experimentation with life styles. In these areas, cautious experimentation may be valuable, but any major change from the social and economic norm of contemporary society must be considered carefully, and individuals involved must freely choose such options with adequate understanding of their implications.

Within charismatic communities, leadership inevitably emerges. Any organized society requires leadership, and its emergence is a sign of growth. There is, however, in such tight-knit communities a danger of confusion between social, economic, organizational, political and spiritual authority. Charismatic communities are in many cases social and political realities and must govern themselves. In a voluntary civil community within a democratic state, individuals can submit themselves to a common order and invest their leaders with considerable authority. The basis of this authority is the individual's free consent. In its exercise, practical and policy decisions will need to be made for the good of the entire group. There is also a spiritual authority which attends leadership in a Christian community. In fact, the leaders of such a community have a certain spiritual authority which is spontaneously acknowledged and are able to exert considerable influence over the lives of their members. Where this authority is responsibly exercised, there is nothing improper about it. It must, however, be distinguished from the authority of the official leaders of the Church. The texts of Scripture which underscore the importance of community order and authority are primarily in reference to the official leadership of the Christian community. Where a community freely chooses to vest its leadership with considerable authority, its basis is the belief and free consent of the members to such government as an appropriate way of serving God and doing his will at that time. Such communities cannot point legitimately to any mandate which gives them any authority over anyone beyond his free consent. Charismatic communities cannot, for example, read into Scripture a blanket endorsement of their life or government without acknowledging the important differences. Even more so, the moral and spiritual influence of the community must not be used to intimidate its members or to equate God's will with that of the community in a way that does violence to participants in the community. Since such communities attract many individuals who are not psychologically strong, a profound respect for the free will of an individual is paramount. That is not to say that the community must decide to live by the principle of the least common denominator. Rather, it must candidly set forth its choices as one alternative way of living out Christ's message and permit individuals to choose freely and without pressure. These distinctions are very important in situations where leaders of charismatic communities are able to exercise greater actual authority than that claimed by the hierarchy of the Church or the leaders of the state.

The elements necessary to form vital community converge in the charismatic renewal. The charismatic experience provides an impetus and basis for community. Most charismatic communities quickly develop leadership, a vehicle for group worship and expression (the prayer meeting), teaching, and a teaching apparatus. The possession of these traits signifies that they are communities. As communities, they can either become mature elements of the Church and society or degenerate into extreme and fanatical sects lost in their own life and practice. These traits do not necessarily endanger the group's unity with the Church. The spirit in which the life of a given community unfolds, especially in its teaching and relations with the hierarchy, will determine its role in the Church.

For these communities to grow in union with the Church, affirmative steps must be taken. Union with the Church is not something to be affirmed once a year or so. A true relationship between communities and the Church must be a living one. The community must drink deeply of the life and teaching of the Church, especially in the sacramental order, through the ministry of ordained ministers and through the teaching of the bishop. Such a relationship requires hard work and really needs to be considered a primary goal of the community if it is to be achieved.

Charismatic community is a powerful phenomenon within the charismatic renewal. It is something which works, and community is an idea which has come into its own. As a conceptual understanding of community is elaborated, however, it is important that it be adequate and balanced. There is a danger of drinking too heady a draught of the ideal of community and seeing it as a panacea for all the problems of the world. The charismatic renewal is still very young. Charismatic communities are also young and have many crises still to weather. It remains to be seen if they can survive the generation which founded them, for example. Furthermore, in their government, life style, and order they have much to learn from the examples of other communities and from various disciplines. There is a pioneering spirit which inevitably tends to want to rethink everything in light of the charismatic dimension. Unless the tendency is balanced by a sober evaluation of the limitations of the charismatic renewal and charismatic communities' ability to be guides and teachers for themselves, it can be narrow and potentially dangerous. Furthermore, in working out an understanding of the charismatic community, there must be a candid recognition of the freedom of individuals to choose the level of community association they wish.

There is a natural tendency to seek to establish models of community. Such a tendency is misdirected. Models are appropriate for engineering or the like, but a community is a living social organism. There are laws and principles which can be formulated regarding community, but to set up a "model" of community would be a serious disservice. Charismatic community is not a universal ideal but a patterned response to the needs of living out the Gospel. Specific communities in some fashion take on the character of the Church, for their members are vessels of salvation. But the form, depth, and extent of community life must be ordered to the needs of the situation. A hierarchy of community which equates an intense form of community with a better form of community, for example, is wrong and absurd, as those outside the renewal can see immediately. Teaching on the value of community in the renewal must avoid extreme over-emphasis of the value of community precisely in order to preserve its real value for the Church.

An individual receiving the charismatic experience must seriously consider the role of Christian community in his or her life. To some extent, everyone who is baptized into Christ is called to participate in the community of Christians. A living Christianity and loyalty to the Spirit, however, often calls for a more immediate involvement with others in a Christian context than is generally possible. Local and immediate communities are a wonderful means of participating in a Christian community.

An individual should be open to such a possibility, seeking to live in a way that is most pleasing to God. If association with a charismatic community would aid in living a Christian life, it should be seriously considered. Life in community provides a regular opportunity to learn to live a life of love. Charismatic communities are not societies of the elect but groups of sinners linked by a desire to grow in Christ. Life in these communities is marked by a need for forgiveness, straightening out points of dispute, making agreements, and admonishment and correction. Building them requires all the tools necessary for building relationships, including human talents and abilities, charismatic gifts of the Spirit, and especially the fruits of the Spirit.

Where charismatic community is not available or exists only in primitive form, it is necessary to wait upon the Lord. Such communities are a work of the Spirit in a true sense. They require a deep working of God in human hearts. The consent by a number of individuals to attempt to seriously relate to one another is no insignificant matter. By analogy with 1 Peter, such communities are houses made up of living stones in which each member is a stone (1 Pt. 2:5). Stones used to build houses need to be quarried and hewn. There is a time, in the building of communities, when hewing must take place, and rough edges chipped off, before a community can be built. This process takes time, patience, and prayer.

B. Three Concrete Steps to Community

An individual who has received the charismatic experience of the Holy Spirit and is associated with a group will encounter community or the opportunity for community in a number of ways. Here it seems wise to focus specifically on three important elements of charismatic community and seek to offer practical advice: (1) prayer meetings, (2) ministry, and (3) forming friendships.

(1) Prayer Meetings

Prayer meetings are the most characteristic activity of the charismatic renewal. These spontaneous assemblies for worship and sharing have marked the renewal from its outset. For many charismatics they represent their first personal involvement in worship. They are for all charismatics an important means of public prayer. They represent, so to speak, a charismatic school of prayer. Because these meetings are so vital for charismatic Christianity and because they shape the lives, attitudes and spirituality of its members, they deserve serious attention. They are important in the spiritual life of an individual, as we have noted in Chapter 3. They are addressed here because they are the focal point for charismatic community, the activity which in some sense defines charismatic community and around which it forms. Prayer meetings therefore represent an important step toward community. A prayer meeting is a joint project between God and a group of individuals, and it can be good or not so good. Because a good meeting is important and because every meeting can be helped when its participants understand it and participate intelligently, we will consider the nature and purpose of a prayer meeting.

(a) The Purpose of a Prayer Meeting

Prayer meetings have a purpose. Often religious activities are taken for granted, and it is assumed that they have intrinsic merit and fit somehow into some cosmic plan. In fact, by failing to specifically define their purpose and articulate expectations, they are often taken less seriously than most other activities in life. Every significant activity, of course, is measured against expectations whether conscious or unconscious. By articulating expectations, the meaning of a prayer meeting can be enhanced. The prayer meeting is an activity which deserves serious treatment.

In order to understand its purpose, it is necessary to view it as one factor in the Christian life. All the activities which a person undertakes to draw closer to God work together with his plan for one's life and for the Church. Regular weekly attendance at a prayer meeting vitally affects the quality of our whole life. It should upgrade the quality of one's Christian life in a significant way. Once it is realized that prayer meetings should make a difference, it also becomes apparent that the quality of a meeting can be judged by its effect on our Christian life. A prayer meeting with much "smoke and thunder" which does little to cause its participants to grow in faith, hope, and love is deficient despite the fireworks. For the same reason, a quiet meeting which results in little growth is deficient, too. Understood in this broader context, it is possible to formulate specific objectives for prayer meetings. The prayer meeting is an assembly for informal public prayer whose purpose is to deepen the Christian life of the entire group and its members through worship, the proclamation of God's Word, and encouragement.

Jesus is present at a prayer meeting in a special way. He promised: "Where two or three are gathered in my name, there am I in the midst of them" (Mt. 18:20). Jesus is in the midst of a prayer meeting. He acts to draw the group together in his presence. Because he is present, worship is especially important at a prayer meeting. The most appropriate response to Jesus' presence is worship. The entire meeting should be ordered toward him and every part should contribute to his worship. The elements of the meeting should be ordered toward worship, not in an abstract sense, but in an intimate and personal sense; the meeting should be a situation in which each person and the whole group are drawn to the worship of God.

A prayer meeting is also a place where God's Word is spoken and obeyed. The Word of God in Christ is a living reality. Through his Word, God calls men more deeply into his life. This Word applies not only to the meeting itself but to the life of the individual and the group. This Word is something which requires active assent on the part of those who hear it. God's Word can be spoken through almost any element of a prayer meeting, but is proclaimed especially through prophecy and Scripture. It is important that a meeting be directed toward listening to the Word which God wishes to speak.

The prayer meeting is also a situation in which the group and its members can be encouraged in their commitment to Christ and living the Christian life. A prayer meeting should contribute to the resolve of its members to live their whole life in Christ and should

encourage them in their efforts. Specific parts of the meeting
should be explicitly encouraging to at least some of them in some
way.

If, at the conclusion of a prayer meeting, the participants have
not been drawn to worship God, heard his Word and applied it to
their lives, and been encouraged, the prayer meeting has failed in
some fashion. All of the elements which characterize a prayer
meeting, such as the charismatic gifts, common prayer, song, sharing, etc., may be operative, but they do not insure a good meeting.
At a good prayer meeting, all the elements work together to draw
the participants to God in worship, through his Word, and by encouragement. A meeting or parts of it can be evaluated in light of
these criteria. For example, if many things were said about worship or people were told to worship, but there was no worship and
the group was not drawn together in worship, the meeting would
be deficient. A good prayer meeting is a place where worship
occurs. The form through which worship occurs does not matter
greatly. Because of the informal nature of a prayer meeting, its
form could vary from singing in tongues to praying a litany. What
matters is that the entire group and its members be drawn in an
act of lifting their hearts toward God in praise. If, by the end of
the meeting, people's hearts have been moved toward God, worship has occurred and the meeting will have accomplished one of
its purposes. Another example would be hearing God's Word. God
has something to say to the group and to individuals. It is important that his Word be spoken. Again, his Word can be spoken in a
number of ways, but it is crucial that it be spoken. If, at the end of
the meeting, individuals and the group have not heard something
from God and made an attempt or decision to obey it, the prayer
meeting has been deficient. Prophecy is an element through which
God's Word *can* be spoken. Yet if there are seven prophecies
which speak the same message, however bland it may seem, and
the attention of the group is not focused on this message in some
clear manner, they are of little purpose. It is not enough that the
prophecies be spoken. Where the prophecy does not command the
attention of the group, some means must be employed such as an
exhortation by which individuals can be helped to concentrate
upon the meaning of God's Word for their lives and encouraged to

formulate a resolution and act upon it. God does not speak to hear himself talk. He speaks to be heard and obeyed. At a prayer meeting, the entire group and individuals should learn to train themselves to seek to hear, understand, and obey his Word. The criteria can also be applied to evaluating a specific contribution to the meeting. For example, a story which is interesting or cute may be proper in other situations, but at a prayer meeting it is not proper unless it draws everyone closer to God. Furthermore, if a point has been made several times and the group seems to have taken it to heart, it is a mistake to make the same point again just because an individual wishes to say it in a compelling (so he thinks) way. Prayer meetings rarely last more than two hours. After singing, announcements, and other miscellaneous matters, there rarely is more than an hour and a half in which to pray. Each contribution should be judged in light of the limited time. Will it help fulfill the purpose of a meeting? Everyone likes to feel good and to hear emotionally inspiring things. A good prayer meeting, however, is not necessarily one which plays on emotions but one which builds a tone of emotional inspiration. It is one in which all the participants have had an opportunity to surrender themselves more fully to God, to be encouraged, and understand specific ways and means by which he can be better served. A warm inner glow fades away after a few hours. Meetings whose purpose is to give participants a glow or warm feeling inside short-change everyone. It is important to set high goals for a prayer meeting. Each meeting and every part of it should lead to a deeper life of charity. It is important to understand the purpose of a meeting and to work to enable it to achieve its purpose.

(b) A Prayer Meeting Is Led by the Holy Spirit

In a special way, the prayer meeting is an activity in which the Holy Spirit works in cooperation with human spirits to accomplish its purposes. This cooperation between God and man is a delicate and fragile work of beauty which can easily be shattered. God rarely works in such a fashion as to drown out the conscious and intelligent participation of the members of a prayer group. It is a mistake to imagine a prayer meeting as a place in which God mystically taps people on the shoulder and prompts them to speak or act. A prayer meeting is better compared to a chorus in which God works as director to bring forth a beautiful song. Different notes are blended together by his genius in perfect harmony. Inspirations and impulses have a role in prayer meetings, but the work of the Spirit can be sensed in a more certain fashion. The Spirit works in a prayer meeting to draw the group to the love of God. It is possible to follow the movement of the meeting and to judge its various parts according to this inner criterion of love. If an element works to set a tone in which God can be better loved and praised, it is in order; if not, it is out of order. In this sense, most properly the entire group and each individual should seek to be led by the Spirit.

In another sense, the Spirit leads as well. He inspires people through various leadings. These inspirations, as mentioned in Chapter 4, should be tested. Specifically at a prayer meeting, they should be judged in light of the tone of the meeting, the time, and the direction the leader is setting. They are not always opportune. If it seems reasonable to speak out or act, a person should do so. A prayer meeting should offer an individual freedom to try to learn to discern the movements of the Spirit. Honest feedback from others is important to the health of the group. Otherwise, those with great self-confidence will become bolder, although not necessarily better, and those with little will become ever more timid and the Spirit's work will be frustrated.

Every member of a prayer group seeks to be sensitive and loyal to the Spirit at a prayer meeting. It is important to cultivate this sensitivity and to seek, at the beginning of a meeting, to quiet one's spirit so as to be able to discern the movements of the Holy Spirit.

(c) The Elements of a Prayer Meeting

A prayer meeting is composed of a number of elements. Each has its own dynamic and functions, but, as has been said, all need to be evaluated in light of the specific purpose of the meeting. We will examine some of them specifically: 1. sharing; 2. prayers; 3. silence; 4. exhortation; 5. prophecy; 6. song; 7. themes and patterns; 8. teaching; 9. a leader.

1. *Sharing.* A sharing is a personal narrative. The term is used to describe the process by which members of a group communicate personal experiences in trying to follow Christ which will be a source of encouragement to others. Any group is built up by hearing of the efforts of others. This dynamic is true of charismatics as well. A sharing can be about an event, experience, relationship, or insight, or it can be a testimony. To be helpful, it should be brief, as specific as possible, and to the point. Long, rambling, and irrelevant sharings deaden a meeting. Although sharings have conclusions, they are most aptly drawn individually by the group. A teaching differs from a sharing in that it, too, can use personal example, but it uses it as a point from which to draw broader conclusions, and it uses other techniques, in addition to example, to reinforce them. A sharing should be given at a point in the meeting where it does not disrupt the flow. It should not embarrass anyone or call too much attention to any individual. Its effectiveness depends on the sharer's sensitivity to the needs of the group, the direction of the meeting, and the brevity and clarity with which it is expressed.

2. *Prayer.* The word of prayer is an oral group prayer in which the entire group lift their voices to God, each in his own way. Some may speak in tongues, others in a native tongue and still others remain silent. The word of prayer can be an effective means of enabling the group to turn their hearts in worship to God. It is something which an individual must learn to enter into. It requires a personal movement toward God and an attempt to express prayer orally. It is necessary to learn not to be distracted by others and to concentrate upon God.

Singing in tongues is a variation of the word of prayer. In it, the entire group joins together in a harmony of praise. In both of these exercises, it is important to regard them as prayer and to pray as they unfold. These forms of prayer can be powerful means of expressing the praise of the group. However, their value can be lessened by being used too often or by individuals disrupting the harmony of the group by singing in too loud or distracting a voice.

There is also value in individuals praying aloud spontaneously. Such prayers, when simple and sincere, enable the entire group to enter into the spirit of the prayer. Through the voiced prayer, the sentiments of the entire group are both formed and expressed. It is important, though, that such prayers in fact be prayers to God and not a way of making a point to the group. Such points are better made through another mode, such as teaching.

3. *Silence.* Silence also has value at a prayer meeting. There are times when each individual should be able to ponder what has been said. At other times the group will subside from spontaneous worship to quiet worship. Such moments are precious and should not be checked. On the other hand, long gaps of silence which are not prayerful can be unsettling and can detract from the value of the meeting. When such pauses occur, members of the group should attempt to break them up by speaking or leading a song.

4. *Exhortation.* An exhortation is an oral message which urges the group to action. It is inspirational in tone and usually ordered to calling upon the group to turn more completely to God in some manner. Exhortations are very important. Of course, it must be added that exhortation can be overdone too, in which case there is a hollow play on emotions. They have special value after the Lord has spoken to the group in some fashion. At such times, the entire group can be exhorted to heed the message. It is important for a group to learn to listen to exhortations and to learn to act upon them where appropriate.

5. *Prophecy.* We have considered prophecy at length in Chapter 5. Here it is necessary only to point out its value and role in a prayer meeting. Prophecy is perhaps the best means by which the living Word of God can be spoken at a prayer meeting. Through it, God is able to lead a group in the most delicate and precise ways to turn to him wholeheartedly. For prophecy to be effective, however, there must be great sensitivity to the Spirit on the part of all. The prophet must be open to prophetic inspiration and carefully test that inspiration. Some messages given as prophecy may not be. The tone and character of the meeting will help determine the appropriateness of a prophecy. Once a prophecy is given,

the attention of the meeting should be directed to it if it contributes to the meeting. This task of discernment belongs to those responsible for leading the meeting. Where authentic, a prophecy will serve to turn a group more fully toward God. If a prophecy calls, for example, for specific movements of the heart such as praise or repentance, it may help to make a public statement to that effect. Whatever resolutions seem proper should be made. Only if the group has weighed the word of prophecy will it fully serve its purpose.

6. *Song.* Song is a wonderful means of worship. It enables a group to express itself in a rich way and is itself a means of enabling the group to participate in the very thing expressed by the song. In order to be fruitful, song requires concentration and cooperation. Not every song creates the same effect and not every song is appropriate at every point in a prayer meeting. There are many factors which determine the value of a song for a prayer meeting, including the tone which the song introduces, its tempo, the message, and the ability of the group to sing it and of the musicians to play and lead it. Songs can serve many uses at a prayer meeting. They can be means of transition from one mood to another. They can recall the group to a point or tone. They can deepen and quiet the tone of the group. They can also lead the group to joyous praise. Songs almost always have some effect, whether good or bad. They should therefore be used with great sensitivity. They are not time-fillers, nor should they be used at a prayer meeting just because the group enjoys singing. A community songfest may be a good idea, but the prayer meeting is not the place for it. An individual should regard song as a means of turning his entire being toward God in prayer. Instead of worrying about words or music, we should concentrate upon turning our hearts to God in an act of love and adoration. A person should try to take on the spirit and words of the song as much as possible.

7. *Themes and patterns.* A prayer meeting often has a theme or several themes. These themes can be inferred from the various contributions to the meeting. For example, a meeting can have a theme of repentance. At such a meeting, the major elements which

make up the meeting will all point to repentance. At times the leader or an individual may announce or suggest a theme, and at other times it may emerge. There is no reason a meeting must have a clear theme, and at times the suggestion of one can seem artificial. If pointing to a theme is of help to the group, it should be done; if not, it should not. It should serve as a gentle guide for the direction of the meeting rather than a fixed rule.

Patterns also tend to emerge in the course of the meeting. A pattern is a series of inter-related actions at a prayer meeting occurring in sequence which make a point or create a tone. A song, prophecy, and exhortation together, for instance, which built upon each other would be a pattern. Patterns can contribute to a meeting.

Normally the thrust of the meeting should be toward common worship. As a result, several elements will often work together in such a way as to call forth prayer from the entire group. These patterns of message and praise are important in the unfolding of the meeting. It often takes several elements to provide adequate content for the group to be able to turn to God meaningfully in prayer. It is a mistake to disrupt the unfolding of either pattern with a song or call to pray prematurely. A period set aside for worship also contributes to the success of a meeting. Prayer is not something that a group can suddenly switch into effectively upon command, but is a state which is gradually entered into. An interior disposition of quiet attentiveness is required for listening to a teaching, message, or sharing. As a result, a period of time set aside for worship insures that this state of prayer can be more readily entered into without the group having to arouse itself to attend to a sharing, teaching or message in between short-lived snatches of prayer.

8. *Teaching.* Teaching occurs in many ways at a prayer meeting. Most teaching at a prayer meeting could be classified as either systematic or pastoral. Each has an important role. Pastoral teaching is related to the needs or concerns of the group or individuals in growing in the Christian life. Systematic teaching is concerned with presenting the truths of the faith in an ordered and understandable fashion. Unless pastoral teaching is founded on an ade-

quate systematic base, it will be shallow and weak, and unless systematic teaching enables the group to participate in the truths of which it speaks, it will not be fruitful. Teaching must be in conformity with God's revelation as understood in the Church. Teaching is an important function in a group. Not everyone can or should teach (cf. Jas. 3). If teaching is given by one respected by the group as a teacher or recommended by others, the teaching will be received attentively. In listening, we should seek to hear Christ's voice speaking to us through the message. Specific resolutions might be made when appropriate. Effective teaching will serve as a platform for its listeners to turn more fully to God.

9. *Leadership.* Unless a meeting is very small, there is a need for a leader. While the Holy Spirit must lead the meeting, his leading involves a delicate cooperation with a group of men. And groups require some explicit leadership to bring about order and harmony. The leader of a meeting should attempt to cooperate with the leadings of the Spirit as they are manifested and should make them evident to the entire group through the various means at his or her disposal such as teaching or exhortation. The leader should seek to preserve a prayerful tone and to move the group toward profound worship of God. We should pray for and actively support and assist the leader. A prayer meeting is a group effort, and leadership is only effective if it receives cooperation.

Each of these elements is different, yet each should draw the meeting closer to God. The elements can be used in a mechanical or in a harmful way. Used wisely, though, they can make a prayer meeting an exercise of love. Effective usage requires discipline and experience as well as understanding. These elements are like tools which can be used for an end. It is important to learn how to put them to work at a prayer meeting for God's glory.

(d) Relationship with Other Forms of Prayer

From the perspective in which we normally view events, prayer meetings are separate and distinct. From God's point of view, the Church is engaged in a constant act of praise and worship. Individuals can enter into that great prayer of the Church in many ways. The great prayer of the Church, the Mass, is the most important means of public prayer because it was given to us by Jesus himself as a memorial. When we pray the Mass, we participate in Christ's death and life in a wondrous way in union with the entire Church. The Mass is only one form of prayer, however. Others include the Divine Office—a liturgical prayer similar to the Mass—and devotions such as Benediction or litanies. Prayer meetings are an informal public prayer having great flexibility. They complement other forms splendidly, adding balance to the more formal ones and deriving strength from them in return. Prayer meetings also complement private prayers and devotions, taking strength from the devotional life of their members and in turn strengthening it. Prayer meetings emphasize prayer, and are, in a special sense, schools of prayer for beginners. Through the spontaneous and oral prayer of the group, an individual can be exposed to prayer and deepened in it. Prayer meetings also prepare a person to appreciate the public prayer of the Church. Participants, having experienced the power of corporate prayer, have an intuitive sense for the value of formal prayer.

(e) Attitudes

It is especially important for a person to consider how best to participate in a prayer meeting. Effective participation requires preparation. The best preparation, of course, is a regular and deep life of devotion. Specific preparation for the meeting is helpful, too. During the week, from time to time specific prayers and sacrifices can be made. On the day of the meeting, a special effort should be made to pray for its success. During the day, upsetting events and distractions should be offered to God for his use. Before the meeting begins, a person should dispose himself in prayer and offer the meeting to God. Simplicity of heart and expectation are the attitudes which should be cultivated. It may help to imagine that we are going to spend time with Jesus. As the meeting draws to an end, a person should recall the major points and especially the resolutions he has made. It may even help to briefly note them in writing. In daily prayer during the week, the messages and resolutions should be referred to whenever helpful. Indeed, they can even serve as the object of daily meditation.

The prayer meeting is an important ingredient of charismatic community. Its quality affects and to an extent determines the quality of community life. A prayer meeting must be taken seriously by communities. It should receive study, reflection and prayer. Its quality depends on the loyalty to the Spirit of those present. Ability to sense the Spirit or sensitivity to his leadings is not something that can be switched on for two or three hours a week very effectively. It must be part of a seven-day-a-week program of love. In the context of this "program," the prayer meeting becomes a special act of love which crowns one's relationship with God and neighbor in a delightful way.

(2) Ministry

Ministry or service is an important consequence of a commitment to Christ. Jesus came into the world "not to be served, but to serve" (Mt. 20:28; Mk. 10:45). He called upon his disciples to imitate him in his generosity. They were to give themselves freely and completely in service. The greatest in the Kingdom was to be "the slave of all" (Mk. 10:44). Christ's call of service remains one which every Christian shares. For a Christian, service is a participation in the work of God and, in a special sense, a means of touching Jesus himself. And what is true of Christians individually, is true of Christian communities as well. Service is a special hallmark of Christian community. The members of the community should be noted for their lives of service to one another and to others outside the community. Service is the external sign by which their love of God and neighbor is manifested.

The charismatic experience usually generates generous impulses which lead a person to seek to express his love in service. One obvious outlet for this impulse is service within the charismatic group. Furthermore, the groups themselves, as organized bodies, tend to seek to express their new-found fervor in service. These generous impulses are an important dimension of the charismatic life. They must be encouraged and cultivated. An understanding of their call to minister will deepen the charismatics' response to the Spirit. For charismatic communities to grow, they must become communities of servants.

The ministry of every Christian can be understood in two ways, primary and secondary.

The primary ministry of every Christian is to love as Christ loved. This ministry is fundamental and necessary in the body of Christ. Love of God and neighbor is the very life-blood of the body. It is Christ's insistent command: "This I command you, to love one another" (Jn. 15:17). Without the ministry of love, the body of Christ withers. Whatever office or position in life or in the Church an individual may hold, his primary duty is to seek in every way to serve through love. At the Last Supper, Jesus deliberately set an example of love and service for his disciples. He washed their feet, and he commanded them to wash one another's feet, signifying by this act the intimate, personal, and humble care which is to mark the brotherhood of believers. This way of love is the more excellent way (1 Cor. 13). Functions can occur in the body without love, but they amount to nothing in the end. The love which Christians are called to have for each other rules out pride or ambition. Christians must cultivate a respect for each other and seek to assist one another in serving God in the fullest possible manner as each is called. In St. Paul's analogy some parts of the body are more honorable, others are less so (1 Cor. 12:23). However, all members of the body have one primary function: to love.

It is important for members of a charismatic community to take the call to minister in love seriously. Notions such as "I can't do anything" represent false humility. Everyone can minister in the sense in which we speak. The least gesture done in love touches the heart of Christ. Even a small act like giving a drink of water for Christ's sake has its reward (Mk. 9:41) and can evidently even make the difference between eternal reward and punishment (Mt. 25:35-42). It is necessary to cultivate an awareness of the importance of the ways that others can be served and to reflect upon ways of being of help. This involves growing in consciousness of others and their needs and in sensitivity toward them. It also involves receiving the service of others with forbearance and humility. In allowing others to serve, we enable them to serve Christ. Discernment, of course, is necessary here.

Growing in this primary ministry of love is important. It should underlie every action performed and every movement of the heart. It is necessary that charismatics strive to put on love. It helps at times to talk about service with others who can be of help to us in understanding how to improve and deepen it.

Everyone is called to minister in a secondary sense as well. Each member of the body has specific functions which can be performed. Some of them are temporary while others may define a person's role in the Christian community. In a specific situation such as a prayer meeting, a person may have a specific function or service. In the series of relationships which comprise the prayer community, a person also has some role. There is also a role and responsibility in the family or primary living situation.

In seeking to understand our role in a given community or situation, it is important not to be anxious. A person should prayerfully consider how he or she can best serve, consult with others, and gladly do whatever he or she can, however humble that may be. Over a period of time, this contribution will become more apparent and will deepen.

There are ministries which have been designated in the body of Christ and given certain authority and responsibility. Christ appointed Peter and the apostles and gave them authority in the Church (cf. Mt. 16:18-20). They, in turn, appointed bishops and elders in the various churches. Gradually other offices came into being to meet various needs. The New Testament offers an example of this process in the story in Acts of the seven deacons. Gradually the order in the life of the Church came to include three offices: bishop, priest, and deacon. In addition to these formal ministries in the Church, there are various spontaneous ministries of service and leadership. In charismatic communities, designated leadership is an important means of harmony for the community. These leaders are designated in various ways. However designated, if they command the support of the community, they should be respected and assisted. Leadership in charismatic communities should understand its responsibility to the shepherds of the Church and also to the members of the charismatic community.

As a charismatic community deepens the understanding of its

members in their call to service and equips them for this service, it will grow. An awareness of ministry is a fundamental element in the creation of a community. By concentrating upon it, charismatics will move toward the formation of substantial communities of love.

(3) Forming Friendships

Friendship is an important part of life. It introduces a quality into life which makes it human in the truest sense. In the sense we speak of it here, friendship is a special voluntary relationship. Of course, in our life we will be involved in many relationships, and each must be governed by charity. However, we will be able to pursue some relationships. These relationships are important in that they shape us and our ideals. It is truly said that a person can be known by his friends.

As a result, the friendships into which a Christian enters are important. They will either build up his love of Christ or undermine it. It is normal for those who have received the charismatic experience to form friendships with one another. This tendency is a major factor in the formation of charismatic communities.

To be effective, a charismatic community must be an organic union of many relationships and friendships. Limitations of time and energy prevent single people or couples from forming friendships with many people. Some specific friendships should be pursued, however. Single individuals should seek to associate with those who will provide companionship and support in the Christian life. Married couples should first be sure that their relationship with each other is a Christian friendship. They also should seek the friendship of other Christians. A prayer group does not have to have households of people living together or close geographical proximity to be able to grow toward community. It does need people who are friends. These little cells will strengthen the entire community and lay the basis for future growth.

Friendships are pursued gradually. Opportunities to come to know one another should be sought, first of all, at common functions, and then through specific meetings. The relationship should not be overly pious. By enjoying activities together, a relationship can deepen. However, Christ should have an important place in the relationship and there should be some occasions for some form of prayer together. By seeking to strengthen and encourage one another in commitment to Christ, Christian friendships can be a vital step toward community. No special gifts are required to form friendship, and simple tools such as the telephone can readily facilitate it. Through prayer and reflection, friendships can be formed, and through love and attention, they can be cultivated. They are an important feature of Christian love and Christian community.

Communities are not built overnight. There are many factors involved in forming communities and they raise many questions. They require cooperation between God and men and between men and other men. Communities which have considerable organization and structure and provide special support are possible and do exist in some form in the charismatic renewal. This kind of community requires considerable effort and sacrifice. It is not available to everyone, nor is everyone called to it. Community in the broader and proper sense, however, is available to all. The charismatic experience opens an individual to community and links individuals together in a common interest. From this common experience, charismatic communities can arise. They require much sacrifice and toil and many years. Love of others is not an easy business for anyone. For it to happen in and through community is even harder. Three ingredients of community which every charismatic can work at, whatever his or her situation, are prayer meetings, ministry and friendships. Through seeking to love in and through these elements, growth in community will be hastened. Furthermore, and what is more important, love will be taking place.

NOTES

CHAPTER I

1. The history and impact of this movement are analyzed in a number of works. *They Speak with Other Tongues* by John Sherrill provides a good introduction to the general reader. Fr. Edward O'Connor's thorough and sensitive study of the movement, recently revised and updated, *The Pentecostal Movement in the Catholic Church*, is by far the best analysis of the movement and its implications.

2. This matter is treated at greater length in my pamphlet, *The Charismatic Experience of the Holy Spirit* (Dove Publications, Pecos, New Mexico). This pamphlet also provides a theoretical background for the entire chapter.

3. For some helpful reflections on the interpretation of history, see the work of J. Maritain, *On the Philosophy of History*, and the numerous works of C. Dawson.

4. For a scholarly and interesting study of this episode, see E. E. Y. Hales' *Napoleon and the Pope*.

CHAPTER III

1. Cf. Yves Congar, O.P., *Lay People in the Church* (Paramus, N.J.: Newman Press, 1967), pp. 312-323. This section offers a thorough examination of this complicated issue.

2. Pius XII, *Divino Afflante Spiritu*, n. 49. In his teaching on Scripture, as in many other areas, Pius XII laid the foundation for much of the work accomplished in Vatican II.

3. *Ibid.*, n. 51.

4. *Constitution on Divine Revelation*, n. 9. It will be obvious that much of this material paraphrases nn. 7-10 of this constitution.

5. Dom Celestin Charlier, *The Christian Approach to the Bible* (Paramus, N.J.: Newman Press, 1965), p. 21. This book is intended as a guide for Christians interested in seriously reading Scripture and is excellent.

6. Pius XII, *Divino Afflante Spiritu*, n. 34.

7. A basic bibliography would include these works by J. McKenzie: *The Two Edged Sword* (about the Old Testament), *The Power and the Wisdom* (about the New Testament), and *Dictionary of the Bible* (a handy reference tool).

8. Others of importance in certain areas for the charismatic are, *Constitution on the Sacred Liturgy*, *Decree on Ecumenism*, *Constitution on Divine Revelation*, and *Constitution on the Church in the Modern World*.

CHAPTER VI

1. In using the Clementine epistles, I do not mean to dismiss the problems which they raise in this context. Because this is not a scholarly treatise, I have used them in accord with one legitimate interpretation and will merely note that some scholars would take issue with it.

RECOMMENDED READING

1. *On the Spiritual Life*: I would encourage anyone recently embarking on a serious Christian life to examine one of the following books and, if helpful, to use it: *Autobiography* of St. Teresa of Avila, *Introduction to the Devout Life* by St. Francis de Sales, and *Imitation of Christ*. While it is impossible to give a blanket recommendation to any book, these three offer an enormous wealth of spiritual wisdom which has been recommended by the Church, having been tested and found to be instruments of grace. The *Spiritual Exercises* of St. Ignatius should be added to this list although they are exercises rather than a book and are best used with a director.

2. *Spiritual Readings*: The following books are a few among many which can give consolation and encouragement to us in our pursuit of God. They are well worth reading and many will be read and reread over the years, for example, *Autobiography* of St. Thérèse of Lisieux, *Practice of the Presence of God* by Brother Lawrence, and *Little Flowers* of St. Francis of Assisi. The works of C. S. Lewis such as *The Great Divorce, The Screwtape Letters*, and *Mere Christianity* are highly beneficial, as is *Who Is Jesus?* by Pope Paul VI. Many works which have come out of the renewal are also valuable, such as M. Basilea Schlink's *Realities* and Watchman Nee's *Release of the Spirit*. Catholic charismatic literature, though newer, can also be helpful—for example G. Martin's pamphlets *Growing in the Spirit* and *Following Jesus*.

3. *Study: Theology for Today* by C. Davis provides a good introduction to theology, as does Frank Sheed's *Theology and Sanity*, though the latter is out of print. As mentioned in the text, McKenzie's books offer a good introduction to scripture. A short four-part series published by the Archdiocese of Chicago is perhaps more suitable for the lay reader. Written by Fr. D. Lupton, it is called *A Guide to Reading the Bible* and is available from

ACTA Publications, 1412 Irving Park Road, Chicago, Illinois. Another book well worthy of the educated layman is J. Maritain's *The Peasant of the Garonne*. In this book the sage sets forth his understanding of the state of the Church in our times. Of course, the *Documents of Vatican II* should head any study list.

Although many other valuable works have not been mentioned, this list has been carefully chosen with the assurance that the reader who trusts himself to it will be in good hands.

APPENDIX

Address of Pope Paul VI to Congress
of Catholic Charismatic Renewal

Dear sons and daughters, in this Holy Year you have chosen the city of Rome for your third international congress. You have asked us to meet you today and to speak to you: in so doing you wished to show your attachment to the Church instituted by Jesus Christ and to everything that this See of Peter represents for you. This concern to take your place clearly in the Church is a genuine sign of the action of the Holy Spirit. For God became man in Jesus Christ, of whom the Church is the Mystical Body, and it is in her that the Spirit of Christ was communicated on the day of Pentecost, when He descended on the Apostles gathered in the "upper room", "devoting themselves to prayer", "with Mary the mother of Jesus" (cf. Acts 1, 13-14).

As we said in the presence of some of you last October, the Church and the world need more than ever that "the miracle of Pentecost should be continued in history" (*L'Osservatore Romano*, English edition, 24 October 1974). In fact, modern man, intoxicated by his conquests, has ended up by imagining that, according to the expressions of the last Council, he is "an end unto himself, the sole artisan and creator of his own history" (*Gaudium et spes*, 20, 1). Alas! to how many, even of those who continue, by tradition, to profess His existence, and, out of duty, to pay Him worship, has God become a stranger in their lives?

"Spiritual Renewal" Testimony

Nothing is more necessary for such a world, more and more secularized, than the testimony of this "spiritual renewal", which we see the Holy Spirit bring about today in the most diverse regions and environments. Its manifestations are varied: deep communion of souls, close contact with God in faithfulness to the commitments undertaken at baptism, in prayer that is often community prayer, in which each one, expressing himself freely, helps, supports and nourishes the prayer of others, and, at the basis of everything, a personal conviction. This conviction has its source not only in instruction received by faith but also in a certain experience of real life, namely that without God, man can do nothing, that with him, on the contrary, everything becomes possible. Hence this need of praising Him, thanking Him, celebrating the marvels that He works everywhere around us and in us. Human existence finds again its relationship with God, what is called the "vertical dimension", without which man is irremediably mutilated.

Not, of course, that this quest for God appears as a desire for conquest or possession; it is a genuine welcome of Him who loves us and freely gives Himself to us, wishing, because He loves us, to communicate to us a life that we receive gratuitously from Him, but not without humble faithfulness on our part. And this faithfulness must be able to unite action and faith according to the teaching of St. James: "For as the body apart from the spirit is dead, so faith apart from works is dead" (Jas 2, 26).

How then could this "spiritual renewal" be other than a blessing for the Church and for the world? And, in this case, how could we fail to take all means in order that it may remain so?

Fidelity to Inspiration

The Holy Spirit, dear sons and daughters, will indicate these means to you, according to the wisdom of those whom He Himself made "guardians to feed the church of the Lord" (Acts 24, 28). For it was the Holy Spirit that inspired St. Paul with certain precise directives, which we will merely recall to you. Fidelity to them will be for you the best possible guarantee for the future.

You know how highly the Apostle esteemed "spiritual gifts": "Do not quench the Spirit", he wrote to the Thessalonians (1 Th. 5, 19), adding immediately: "test everything; hold fast what is good" (*ibid*. 5, 21). He deemed, therefore, that discernment was always necessary, and he entrusted control to those he had put at the head of the community (*ibid*. 5, 12). With the Corinthians, some years later, he goes into more detail: in particular, he points out to them three principles in the light of which they will be more easily able to carry out this indispensable discernment.

Authentic Doctrine

The first one, with which he begins his exposition, is faithfulness to the authentic doctrine of the faith (1 Cor. 12, 1-3). Anything contradicting it cannot come from the Holy Spirit: he who distributes his gifts is the same one who inspired the Scriptures and who assists the living Magisterium of the Church, to which, according to the Catholic faith, Christ has entrusted the true interpretation of Scripture (cf. Constitution *Dei Verbum*, n. 10). That is why you feel the need of a more and more thorough doctrinal formation: biblical, spiritual and theological. Only such a formation, the authenticity of which must be guaranteed by the Hierarchy, will preserve you from deviations, always possible, and will give you the certainty and the joy of having served the cause of the Gospel "without beating the air" (1 Cor. 9, 26).

Love Above All

The second principle. All spiritual gifts are to be received gratefully; and you know that the list given is a long one (1 Cor. 12, 4-10, 29-30), without claiming to be complete (cf. Rom. 12, 6-8; Eph 6, 11). However, granted "for the common good" (1 Cor. 12, 7), they do not all procure it to the same degree. Thus the Corinthians must "earnestly desire the higher gifts" (*ibid*. 12, 31), those most useful to the community (cf. *ibid*. 14, 1-5).

The third principle is the most important one in St. Paul's mind. It has inspired one of the finest pages, without doubt, in all literature, to which a recent translator has given an evocative title: "Love soars above everything" (E. Osty).

However desirable spiritual gifts may be—and they are—only the love of charity, *agape*, makes the perfect Christian, it alone makes man "pleasing to God", "gratia gratum faciens", as the theologians say. For this love does not merely presuppose a gift of the Spirit; it implies the active presence of his Person in the heart of the Christian. Commenting on these verses, the Fathers of the Church vie with one another in explaining it. According to St. Fulgentius, to quote only one example, "the Holy Spirit can confer all kinds of gifts without being present himself; He proves, on the contrary, that He is present through grace, when He grants love", "se ipsum demonstrat per gratiam praesentem, quando tribuit caritatem" (*Contra Fabianum*, Fragment 28; P.L. 65, 791). Present in the soul, He communicates, with grace, the very life of the Holy Trinity, the same love with which the Father loves the Son in the Spirit (cf. Jn. 17, 26), the love with which Christ loved us and with which we, in our turn, can and must love our brothers (cf. Jn. 13, 3), "not in word or speech but in deed and in truth" (1 Jn 3, 18).

By Its Fruits

Yes, the tree is judged by its fruits, and St. Paul tells us that "the fruit of the Spirit is love" (Gal. 5, 22), such as he described in his hymn to love. It is to love that are ordained all the gifts that the Holy Spirit distributes to whom He wills, for it is love that builds up (cf. 1 Cor. 8, 1), as it was love that, after Pentecost, made the first Christians a community "devoted to the apostles' teaching and fellowship" (Acts 2, 42), "all having one heart and soul" (*ibid*. 4, 32).

Be faithful to these directives of the great Apostle. And according to the teaching of the same Apostle, be also faithful to the frequent and worthy celebration of the Eucharist (cf. 1 Cor 11, 2-29). It is the way chosen by the Lord so that we may have his Life in us (cf. Jn 6, 53). Likewise, too, approach confidently the sacrament of reconciliation. These sacraments tell us that grace comes to us from God, through the necessary mediation of the Church.

Dear sons and daughters, with the help of the Lord, fortified by the intercession of Mary, mother of the Church, and in communion of faith, charity and apostolate with your Pastors, you will be sure not to make a mistake. And thus you will make your contribution to the renewal of the Church.

Jesus is the Lord! Alleluia!

Pope's Speech in English

We are happy to greet you, dear sons and daughters, in the affection of Christ Jesus, and in his name to offer you a word of encouragement and exhortation for your Christian lives.

You have gathered here in Rome under the sign of the Holy Year; you are striving in union with the whole Church for renewal —spiritual renewal, authentic renewal, Catholic renewal, renewal in the Holy Spirit. We are pleased to see signs of this renewal: a taste for prayer, contemplation, praising God, attentiveness to the grace of the Holy Spirit, and more assiduous reading of the Sacred Scriptures. We know likewise that you wish to open your hearts to reconciliation with God and your fellowmen.

For all of us this renewal and reconciliation is a further development of the grace of divine adoption, the grace of our sacramental Baptism "into Christ Jesus" and "into his death" (Rom. 6, 3), in order that we "might walk in newness of life" (v. 4).

Importance of Baptism

Always give great importance to this Sacrament of Baptism and to the demands that it imposes. Saint Paul is quite clear: "You must consider yourselves dead to sin but alive to God in Christ Jesus" (v. 11). This is the immense challenge of genuine sacramental Christian living, in which we must be nourished by the Body and Blood of Christ, renewed by the Sacrament of Penance, sustained by the grace of Confirmation and refreshed by humble and persevering prayer. This is likewise the challenge of opening your hearts to your brethren in need. There are no limits to the challenge of love: the poor and needy and afflicted and suffering across the world and near at hand all cry out to you, as brothers and sisters of Christ, asking for the proof of your love, asking for the word of God, asking for bread, asking for life. They ask to see a reflection of Christ's own sacrificial, self-giving love—for his Father and love for his brethren.

Yes, dear sons and daughters, this is the will of Jesus: that the world should see your good works, the goodness of your acts, the proof of your Christian lives, and glorify the Father who is in heaven (cf. Mt. 5, 16). This indeed is spiritual renewal and only through the Holy Spirit can it be accomplished. And this is why we do not cease to exhort you earnestly to "desire the higher gifts" (1 Cor. 12, 31). This was our thought yesterday, when on the Solemnity of Pentecost we said: "Yes, this is a day of joy, but also a day of resolve and determination: to open ourselves to the Holy Spirit, to remove what is opposed to his action, and to proclaim, in the Christian authencity of our daily lives, that Jesus is Lord".